LIVING *in a* CO-OP *and the* JOURNEYS *to* COURT

Van Hugo

authorHOUSE®

AuthorHouse™
1663 Liberty Drive
Bloomington, IN 47403
www.authorhouse.com
Phone: 1 (800) 839-8640

Published by AuthorHouse 12/29/2017

ISBN: 978-1-5462-2330-6 (sc)
ISBN: 978-1-5462-2329-0 (e)

Print information available on the last page.

This book is printed on acid-free paper.

Part 1

History

When I came to New York on November 15, 1996, it was very cold that night. I thought I would have a normal and simple life in the city, particularly living in a good place. My father and my older brother came to get me at the airport. As I entered in the building for the first time, there were group of males playing cards or dominos (If I remembered about which one of the games they were playing). We did not say hello to them, and they did not say hello to us as well. As I entered in the apartment 2D for the first time, I was a little shocked about the apartment. The apartment looked very old. The floors in the apartment, including the bathroom floor and the kitchen floor covered with regular tiles. The bathroom floor and the kitchen floor were in bad shape than any other floors in the apartment. My older sister happened to be the one opened the apartment's door when we came in that night. When I headed in the kitchen, and the light turned on, I saw my father picked up a knife a huge; rushing to kill roaches with the knife. He killed as many as he could that night. Who knew for how long my father had been doing that until it faded away.

I began to pay attention later on to other problems in the apartment such as mice, ceilings, and holes problems. Killing mice in the apartment was like committed genocide. We had no choice because mice could get on our food, as well as caused health issues for us. When mice got on our food, we have no choice, but threw the food away. I do not know for how long the mice issue had been going on before I came to the apartment at the end of 1996. The mice problem had been going on a daily basis since I moved in the apartment at the end of 1996 until the illegal eviction that occurred on September 29, 2014. We probably killed more than thirty mice in the apartment. I do not know about how may mice the others killed. In my part, I lost count, but I killed more than a dozens of mice in the apartment from the year 1996 until the illegal eviction that took place in 2014. The mice issues and problems got worse because the mice happened to be everywhere. The mice issues and problem got worse after the fire that took place in the apartment above us on the holyday in February 2006. The mice began to be in places that they never been before. I began to hear mice through the ceiling. I also began to see them coming out of the holes on the floor that are in the living room, bedroom, and kitchen.

There was no good work done in the apartment above us after the fire in 2006. There was no good work done in our apartment after the fire as well. The ceiling in the living room was in the worse condition than the other ceilings in the apartment before the fire occurred. When the tenant who lived above us (which was a shareholder) got drunk and had spilled going on in his apartment, it came straight down to us without delay. I could say that the tenant above us had not only drinking problem. Even though we came from the same country, that does not mean we had to take responsibility and/or blame for his drunkenness. What to worry about was the type of substances came down to us. These substances could either be alcohol or urine. I used to hear the tenant footsteps when he came in his apartment, especially when he was drunk and had his bottles collapsing on the floor. The tenant above was also a smoker. When the spills came down to us, it came down to us near where the light bulb located. The urine spill was the worse because it had strong and powerful odor. I do not know if the tenant above us used to store urine in containers or bottle for a short or long period of time. I remembered one night I came from to work; the tenant had his urine came down and landed on the back of my neck. I was very pissed off. I decided to go to his apartment and knocked on his door so loud. This was not the first time my brother and I knocked on the tenant's door when we fed up with the disgusting spills. The tenant never came to open his apartment's door when that happened.

One day my older brother went to knock on the tenant apartment's door with steel that was about twenty to thirty inches' long. My brother slammed the steel so hard on the door. The tenant never responded. One day we called the police on the tenant. The police did not do anything about the problem that we reported to them. The police just went and knocked on the tenant's door and that was the only thing they did. When the police came back to us, they said that was all they could do. On the day the fire occurred that February 2006, it was a disaster for us. The ceiling in the living room happened to get affected the worse because that was where the fire actually started. What started the fire had been remained unknown to us. My brother and I knew of the fire because we use to sleep in the living room. My sisters used to sleep in the other room which was not a bedroom but only part of the kitchen. Therefore, six of us used to live in one-bedroom apartment. My mother came to the country in a month after I came in in 1996. My oldest sister came in the country in 1999. My oldest sister lasted two years in the apartment, got married, and has life of her own. My older sister and my older brother came in the country 1996 as well. We all had our paper works done at the same time. However, there was a problem for some of us. My older sister and older brother had everything done for them at the American Embassy in Haiti. They happened to be the first one who got their paper works done. My mother and I were delayed on our paper works. We had specific date to come back at the embassy for that. My oldest sister had it worst because her problem seemed to be about her age. My older sister got married, live the apartment after probably seven years later. My older sister got married probably three years after my oldest sister marriage. It was my brother and I left in the apartment. On the day of the fire in February 2006, my sisters were not there.

We knew something was wrong that night when we saw pile of water dripping down on us so fast in many spots, particularly about new spots. It was surprised that water came down from other spots in the living room's celling. That happened for the first time. We knew about one spot, not other spots. It was always risky for us to eat food in the living room. We were waiting like we usually did after the substance came down to us, stopped dripping, took a mop to mop it, and move on with our life. That night water never stopped dripping. My brother and I decided to go up to the tenant's apartment. My brother was closer to the tenant's apartment. As we got near to the front of the apartment, we saw smoke came out of the apartment. The apartment's door was still closed while smoke came out. My brother knocked on the door to find out if everything was fine. The tenant responded by saying yes, everything was fine from the inside without opened the door. My brother and I could hear loud noises went on in the apartment, as if someone was in trouble. We did hear noises went on above us, as well while water dripping down on us, before we went up to the tenant's apartment. The noise was more of our concerned because the noise was different from any other noises that the tenant used to make before. The apartments are echoes and the building that we living in are

3

echoes as well. Any small noises that happened in the building and the apartment above us counted as big noises.

When we found something was wrong and the tenant's apartment was under fire, we decided to knock on almost everyone's door and called out loud "fire". Everyone heard us and got out. The tenant was intoxicated while the fire occurred in the apartment. How did I know about that? When he did not respond properly when we knocked on his door before the fire got worse. His speech was more like of someone who had been drinking. Another reason to prove he was drinking was when the Fire Department had to break in the apartment to kill the fire and got him out. The Firemen had to cover him with a blanket because he was naked (except his underwear was on). The firemen had to carry him out. The water that dripping down on us justified enough that the tenant tried to put out the fire all by himself. This was not the first fire that fire occurred in both buildings ever since I live in the building in 1996. I witnessed about four fire situations in b buildings from the year 1996 to the year 2010. All of these fires that occurred may have seemed to remain unknown what really started them. However, the last fire that took place on July 5, 2010 was kind of known about it. There were stories or rumors about the fire. I heard the first story about that the fire was caused by firecrackers. I heard that someone must have had threw fire crackers and landed on the roof of the other building. The fire began to be known about when one of the tenants who lived in the apartment discovered it by miracle. The person found out about the fire when she saw smoke out of the window. The fire happened above her where she slept. I went to her apartment along with a neighbor whom we knew who used to come to our apartment, knew the person affected by the fire. They both lived in the same building, and they both Haitians. The neighbor who used to come to our apartment is no longer lived in the other building. He had life of his own. We still see each other once in a while. He still comes in the building because he has relative lives in the building. As I was in the apartment where the fire occurred, the lady explained that she was almost died. I looked above where the fire occurred. The firemen had to break the ceiling open to kill the fire. I could say that the distance between ceiling and the roof was about four feet deep. However, I thought only one apartment affected by the fire. The apartment next door also got affected by the same fire. Another Haitian lives in that apartment as well. These Haitians have been living in the building for over thirty years.

The second story I heard about the fire could possibly be true. During the year 2015, my brother told me that he heard that the July 5th 2010 fire was caused by one of the board's relative and had remained as a secret. The fire may have caused on purpose. What I did about that information is to include it in one of the letters I sent to the Judge who handled the trial of the holdover proceeding case, along with other information and documents. Part one of the book is just a beginning of what will come throughout the book. What has been going in the buildings are scary, deep, ugly, and messy politically, socially, and economically. What has been going in the buildings even get scarier, deeper, uglier, and messier almost from the middle of the year 2008 until the illegal eviction that took place on September 29, 2014. There has been a lot of wrongdoings occurred in the buildings which the people, including my father, who lived in the buildings for over thirty years had to endure. There were also a lot happened during the year 2013 and 2014, which the people who live in the buildings did not know about until I discovered them miraculously; during the time I was in court with the people in charge of the buildings, known as the CO-OP board. The people who control the buildings effectively knew what they have been doing. They screwed the buildings not only for themselves and their families, but also everyone else. They ended up bringing everyone down with them.

The history part is important because it has some connections at what had been going on in the buildings and in court. Above all, there had been a lot of monkey businesses (corruption, extortion, and robbery) going on in the buildings for over thirty years. Dealing with the problems and issues that had been going on in the buildings was super-duper extremely difficult. The rest of the book would be based on them. I always hear some people say do not worry about the past. They are wrong to some degree. However, it depends what to forget or let go off in the past. There are things that happened in the past always going to affect what would happen in the present and the future. The past, present, and future look like some kind of triangular effects and reaction because a lot of situation that happened are concentrated on them. The problems that the CO-OP board committed happen under prejudice, discrimination, carelessness, irresponsible, ignorance, arrogance, harassment, hypocrisy, injustice, and power hungry. The CO-OP board happened to be control by bunch of wicked, nasty, dirty, messy, sneaky, slicky, and sleazy individuals. However, the CO-OP board is not the only one caused problems in the buildings. There are several outsiders who contributed to the problems. These outsiders are the board's lawyer(s), G***** and L*** PLLC and LLP. The others groups which are under suspicious are the Lady at the Private sector and the gentleman at the Public sector, particularly the lady at the Private sector. These people knew some of the wrongdoings that the board has committed, and they never did anything to help out. I made them know more during the time I was in court with the board, especially on the trial of the holdover proceeding, particularly the gentleman at the Public sector.

What the board and their lawyer(s) hand been doing in court and outside of court from the HP action case, small claim case, to the holdover proceeding case was that they have been playing a lot of nasty games. These kinds of games are pretentious, lies, denials, anonymous, deception, diversion, and unpredictable. What had been going on in all of the court cases in court had effect and impact of what had been going on outside of the court. Dealing with the board, board's lawyer(s), Private sector, and Public sector was like I was at war with more than one army at once. The Authority knew about everything that had been going on, as well as everyone included here. It costed me over thirty dollars on mails, to send reports and documents of everything to Authority about what had been going on. I sent four to five yellow envelops and two white envelops fill with documents of what happened. Most of what I sent to Authority had been sent first class mail. Each yellow envelops costed about five dollars each. The board and their lawyer(s) had been keeping me busy for two years. Why there were more than four envelops sent to Authority because all of these envelops contained the outcome of each court case that I have been in. I sent them separately to the Authority. I did not know if things could have got that far. The magnitude of what I had to deal with was enormous. Everything that I sent to Authority, the Housing Court in Downtown Brooklyn had more than half of them. I sent some good amount to the gentleman at the Public sector. As for the Lady at the Private sector, I began to discover that she is on the favor of the board as personal lawyer. I did not send much to her because she was helping the board, as well as contributed to the problems that happened to me. I send all of the documents that the board and the board's lawyer(s) sent to me by mails, and sent them to her by email.

At the end of part one, there would be part of the report I wrote included which I sent to Authority twice. It may continue to be extended one more time because there are few things that needed to be added and fixed. The outcome of what I had to deal with the board considered the board as criminal, mafia, and economic gangsters. The board had been committed financial crime in the buildings for almost thirty years. What I also found so shocking, was that the police were helping the board to some degree. There are more details about that in one of the outcomes of the court cases I include in the book. The finances of the buildings seemed to be in ruin before and during the time the buildings turned into CO-OP in 1988-1989. The buildings should have generated over three million dollars in over thirty years. What happened to the finances of the buildings? What had been going in the buildings for over thirty years may also consider "American Greed". After what happened in court was that the board and their lawyer(s) had the intention to commit fraud, perjury, identity theft, falsify information and documents, as well as committed other problems on purpose. I did what I had to do just to protect myself from all the wrongdoings that the CO-OP board and their lawyer(s) had been committed. I knew what they did on the HP action case, small claim case; particularly about the trial of the holdover proceeding case would effectively have affected the buildings. The board and their lawyer(s), particularly the board's lawyer(s) went against the Judge's decision. The board and their lawyer(s) made things worse for themselves, especially the board's lawyer(s).

There are few things I want to say before the fire that occurred above us on February 2006. We did talk to the tenant when we saw him while sober. We did tell him about the noise problems. He listened and still did not do the best to lower on the noise. The tenant has been living in the apartment above us for over thirty years as well. He used to come to our apartment probably twice. I remembered he said to us that he used to pay rent, but stopped paying because the people who were in charge never come to fix the apartment. He referred to the people in charge as "they" without mentioning anyone's names. He also added that he would start to pay rent when they fixed the apartment. Later on my father said he had made a big mistake at not paying his rent. On the day my father left the apartment, he almost made a huge mistake. That mistake could have had costed him big time, even though it was not going to be his fault. He was going to sell the apartment. That was what he was intended to do. He never said to us to whom he would sell it and who gave him the authorization to sell the apartment. He just kept everything in secrets. We stood in the way because we had nowhere to else to go. My father decided to let me and my mother take responsibility of the apartment without given to us any copies of documents. It was the board who told my father that he could sell the apartment, which was what I discovered before I went to court, filed for HP action against the buildings. If selling the apartment was legal and legit, that was the kind of issue remained a problem for the board and their lawyer(s) on the holdover proceeding case. The board and their lawyer(s) created the problems to themselves which used against them on the holdover proceeding case.

The problems and issues that the board and their lawyer(s) caused, started during the HP action case, continued to the small claim, and met all of the problems and issues on the trial of the holdover proceeding. Few years before the fire occurred above us, I used to hear my father told stories about the buildings. One story was about it was a bunch of families living in both buildings. These families did not want him to live in the building. My father found the apartment by the help of a friend, who was Haitian and happened to live in the other building. That friend was the one and the other tenant who affected by the fire in July 5, 2010, used to stand up against all of the wrongdoings that had been going on in the buildings committed by the board. That friend passed away. What happened to the other tenant (shareholder) would explain in details later on. Another story my father used to say was that he used to find trash in front of the apartment's door. One day my father found candles and other stuff in front of the apartment's door as if someone performed magic spell in front of the door. Another story was about thieves used to come in the apartment almost every day. No wonder why we place cages on all windows to keep the thieves out. The theft issues and problems usually caused by insiders. Few or some of the thieves happened to be relatives of the people who were in charge of the buildings, the board. I do not know if the other Haitians in the buildings used to suffer from the theft problems as well. The tenant above us used to suffer from the theft problem as well.

One of the thieves almost victimized by the tenant's machete few years before the fire occurred in the tenant's apartment on February 2006. That thief happened to be one of the board's relative. One day I was on my way in the apartment, that relative stopped and told me that he disrespected by the tenant above us because the tenant kept calling him thief. One day the tenant came to our apartment explained to us about the theft problems. I was in the apartment that day. I did not remember if my brother and my mother were there. The tenant told me that he had enough with the theft problem because he always had electronic devices stolen by the thief. He said every time he bought something new, the thief stole it. He said that nothing lasted him two days and the theft activities usually happened while he went to work. He was a taxi driver. He said that one day the thief thought he was out. He heard a noise that someone tried to open one of the apartment's windows. He said that he slowly pulled out his machete. He ran toward the thief with the machete. He said he swung the machete at the thief and missed because the thief was still at the window, and had chance to jump down. He said that he almost cut either the thief's head or arms. He also identified the thief. The tenant said he used to make a hand gesture as if he had a machete on his hand, in front of the thief every time he saw the thief. He explained that the hand's gesture was a message that one day he would get the thief if the thief did not stop. However, the tenant died from the drunkenness problem he had to go through, as well as lost his job and the apartment, probably a year and half after the fire occurred in the apartment.

The thieves in the buildings used to have friends in the neighborhood helping them on the theft activities. Placing cages on the windows of the apartment to keep the thieves out was not funding by us. We did pay to have thing fixed in the apartment as well. We put windows, heaters, fixing other broken parts of the apartment with our money while paying rent every month for the apartment. Some of the work that we did in the apartment happened under collaboration from some of our relatives, particularly about placing cages on the windows. We keep fixing things in the apartment since my father moved in the apartment in 1981 and continued to do so until the HP action I filed against the buildings in the middle of the year 2013. I inherited not only the apartment from my father, but also inherited all of the other problems surrounding the apartment and the buildings. These problems are social, political, and economics. What started all of the problems was the damage that occurred on the bathroom floor that I built by level it up in May 2012. A friend of ours, particularly friend of my brother, did the work for us. He was legit, certified, and qualified to do the job for us because he went to school to learn about what he is doing now as career. He knew that he was an outsider, as well as knowing about building rules and regulations when it comes to contractors. We both put together to build the bathroom floor. The bathroom floor remained damage probably since my father moved in the apartment. The bathroom floor remained damage ever since I moved in the apartment since November 1996. Our friend told me that the bathroom floor and the whole bathroom, along with the entire apartment suffered from physical structure problem. As I was doing research online about the building during the time I was in court on the HP action case, and found out that the buildings were built during 1930's. It was quiet evident that there were so much problems going on in the buildings. I paid fees to our friend, which he was very generous to us because he charged me fees that I could afford to some degree. There are more details about everything later in the book because the bathroom situation was used against the board and their lawyer(s) from the HP action case, Small claim case, to the holdover proceeding case, along with other problems and issues as well.

The board and the super damage the bathroom floor on July 2, 2013 and they had the nerve to blame me as the victim, and had the intention to charge me for the damage. What I found out from few other tenants in the buildings, told me that they suffered the same problem that super damaged their properties. The board knew about that and never did anything about these problems. Most of these tenants also happened to be Haitians. One of them happened to live who live in the same building as us. I happened to find out about these problems during the time I was in court on the HP action cases in 2013. I would never know about these problems if I did not go searching to know about them, including every other problems surrounding the buildings. It even scared me about discovering these problems and dark secrets that had been going on in the buildings for over thirty years. The next part would be concluded by representing all the parties involved at what is going in the buildings. The part below sent to Authority, which I omit the identity of for the book. That should be the last extended version of it. I omit the names of the people in charge despite the fact that their names appear in documents that I include in the book. I also did not include the names of the others because I need to prevent unnecessary and unwanted lawsuits against me. I also omitted the name of the others, as well as their organizations. The only thing remains unhidden for the board is their titles.

I face almost the same thing in court just like the tenant who was affected by the July 2010 fire. The tenant told me that the board served her to be in court while she was homeless. She did not know that she was served by the board. Her court case had been expired for few months. She hired a lawyer (her private lawyer) to help her out. She told me that the board tried to change things in court when they got caught on their wrongdoings. The board claimed that they were waiting for the insurance money. The shareholder told me that she received an envelope sent by the board's lawyer. The envelope filled with a lot of false allegation and lies against her. She knew that these false allegations and lies done by the president. I did not ask her that if the court knew about these false allegations and lies, as well as if her lawyer knew about these false allegations and lies, and brought them to the court's attention. She even told that the board's lawyer hated the board. There will be details and cases I have against her lawyer after I was evicted from the apartment illegally, at the end of the book.

• Sent to Authority on January and probably on July 2014 and the updates few months later (send twice)

About the Board and more

The board is comprised of three families: their full names are omitted for the book. I want you to know that the board done a lot of things in secrecy. They are the board of directors and board members. The problems of families taking advantage of other families have been going on for years or decades.

The President: He became president without anyone vote for him, after the CEO, passed away end of May 2008. There was no vote went on for president, based on what one of the shareholders told me. He became president through favoritism by the others. The corporation is located secretly in his apartment in the other building. He also tells me that he puts the apartment that he lives in under his wife's name, after he and others raised the rent by 14% again January 2013. He is the one who signs the receipts every month after the payment made for the apartments. He also claims that he does not live in the apartment. He has his whole family living in his apartment.

Head (Chief): I do not know how long she has been the head officer, but she probably held head officer position for years or decades. She probably has other apartments in other building. Otherwise I may be mistaken about everything. Everyone should see how her apartment looks like now. She fixed everything inside her apartment in 2011, and wondering where she got the money from. Her floor in her apartment changes color at day and at night. She is the one who collects payments in the building I live in. Her and her son also claims that they do not live in the apartment that they live in. She also has the book of the finances of the buildings. She knows who pay for their rent and not. The shareholder who found out about the unfair and illegal rent hikes told me that the head's husband was angry at her when she asked her about the book. She wanted to find out who pay their maintenance or rent. The head also has relative lives in the other building. Her husband passed away early the year 2013.

Manager: I also do not know how long she has been officer and manager as well. The apartment that she lives in the building that I live is under her husband's name. Her parents live upstairs in one of the apartment on the 4th floor. She and her husband probably have relatives living in both buildings. The same shareholder told me that her and another shareholder who passed away in 2007 or 2008, went after her husband, or relative live on the fourth floor, out of the Presidential position due to the reasons of taking power for granted and tried to move more of his relatives in both buildings. It was done by the lady who was affected by the July 5th, 2010 fire and the tenant who passed away. The lady happened to be the one who told me about that. I find out now that it is the Manager who has more relatives living in the buildings.

CEO/Chair: she was the CEO/Chair of the two buildings. I also do not know for how many years or decades she had held her position as a CEO before she passed away end of May 2008. I heard that her son loss the apartment she lived in the other building, due to make up of fake checks or not. I also heard that she was also spent a lot of the buildings money for her personal use before she passed away. It was the others I heard accused the CEO/Chair and her son of such doing and kick the son out of the building. I found that very hypocrisy of the others. The others have been doing the same thing that they claim the CEO/Chair had been doing. However, the CEO/Chair was not dumb and stupid like others to kick people out of the buildings and rented the apartments under their names on sub-letting for over $ 1500 a month. The CEO/Chair knew that the problem of the buildings would soon come back to hunt her and the others in the future. Now wonder the others, beside the President, used to benefit on everything while she was alive. You will be surprised that her name is still in used as the CEO/Chairman of the Buildings. She said that she liked money in front of me few weeks after the fire that occurred in the apartment of one of the shareholder above me (3D) in February 2006.

That apartment had been closed down until her death, as well as opened for rent during the same week of her death. There are a lot of changes that has been going on in the buildings where some of the apartments in both buildings happened to be inhabited by tenants who pay more than $ 1000 a month, after her death. Event some of the tenants suffer from the mice problems, as well as internal physical structure problems in the apartments. Even few or some shareholders are now paying nearly $600 and $ 700 dollars a month in damage apartments, without the light and gas bills included. She never did good work inside the apartments. She never done any good work in the apartment that I live before and after the fire that occurred. Even the others never did any good work inside other shareholders who suffered from the fire that occurred in the other building, in July 2010. One of the shareholders told me that she had to spend 10th of thousands of dollars do redo her floor and her bathroom floor after the fire occurred. The shareholder told me that the board would never do any good jobs in her apartment. The other shareholders who suffered from the fire told me the same thing. These shareholders and I happened to be the one who have been discriminated against in the buildings for decades.

I also do not know how much money had been given on insurance to fix my father's apartment, as well as their apartments after the fires that occurred. Therefore, nothing changes in the buildings for decades. It is now become a myth to live in low rent income housing in the past 6 years. Try to find out how much money the CEO/Chair, left in her account for the buildings after her death. I overheard the president said to a shareholder that she left a sum of $ 100,000 or $ 200,000 in her account, when he convinced the shareholder that he is trying to do something good with it. I was inside the apartment while the conversation took place in front of the apartment's door, probably in year 2011 or 2012. You can hear almost everything in the building I live due to echoes. I just find out that she used to sign receipts and her name is in the Stock Certificate. I just found out about that at the end of November 2014 when I got access to my father documents somewhere else. My father moved out with the buildings' documents with him on the day he left the apartment in 2008, and placed them somewhere. I do not blame him to be very personal, but he should have known that to leave few copies of these documents with us before he left. No wonder why the President asked me about my father's Stock Certificate. I wonder whose name should be in the new Stock Certificate now after the death of the CEO/Chair if there are any new Stock Certificates for every shareholder.

The Bylaws and / or the Proprietary least: I send you the copy of the Bylaws because that is what the board gave me before I went to court. I do not know the beginning, middle, and end of it. The Bylaws is forty pages long, and the same thing has been printing or copied many times to make it more than forty pages. The board themselves do not know what the proprietary least look like. I have to download documents that may appear to be real and legit from the net. I send the copy of the Bylaws for analysis, as well as for investigation. Some of the shareholders told me that they lost their proprietary least at the fire that happened in their apartments. Some said this paper is nearly 30 years old. They found it surprise that the board asking them about a Proprietary Lease that has been there for decades and remained forgotten. That happened due to the reason that the board is in court with me and put it on paper when it is unrelated to the HP action. Any shareholders do not know the reason why the board asked them their proprietary least. The board needs to answer a question how many pages the Bylaws and Proprietary least are. I do not know if the board incorporates the Bylaws and Proprietary least as one. They both were unrelated to the HP action case. I send you the copy of the Bylaws that the board gives to every shareholder or not. I do not know the beginning, the middle, and the end of it as I mentioned before. They board claimed or stated that it is said in the Bylaws and Proprietary Lease that the spouse of the shareholder, as well as the child and any of the relatives of the shareholders shall not inherited the apartment. Does this rule or regulation apply to everyone including themselves or just for non-families only? Which one of them is in used? Can two different sets of rules and regulations apply to a building? Otherwise they will contradict each other. Does anyone need to have proprietary lease for their private houses or properties? That question needs to be answered. I still do not know what a proprietary lease looks like beside the one I found on line.

The lady at the Private sector: She is the assistant at the Private sector. I went to see her at her office located around Wall Street twice. The first time I went to see her, was probably a week after I left court for the first HP action, on August 2013. We sent email to each other before and after I went to see her. The board lied to her about saying that the Judge ruled over me, as well as lying about that I hired unlicensed contractor to build the bathroom floor. I let her knew that the contractor had license. She did not know that my father was absent since 2008 and let my mother and I responsible for the apartment. She thought that my father just left the apartment and never came back. I explained to the reason that my father left had to do to his retirement and health issues. I let her knew that the board knew about that. She said to me it was fine to pay the apartment under my father's name. She also said that the apartment would belong to my mother after my father passes away, if both of my parents stay married. However, she tries to make me feel like some kind of stranger inside the apartment. I went to see her the second time, on September 2013, few days after the inspector came in the apartment. She said that I have been sued. I asked her show me proof of it. I sent her the papers that the board's lawyer sent me. She could not find where it said on the paper that I have been sued, but only false allegations and lies that are on the papers, which only used as prejudice and fear against me, but never brought up in front of the judges. She even said to me that I wasted my time coming to her office because there is nothing she could do for me. She was the one who told me that there are some people taking advantage of my father when I came to see her for the first time. She also said that some people do not pay anything for 20 over years, as well as missed out on the rent. She also said that the Government did not fix all of the apartments in both buildings.

Before I left her office the second time, I asked her about if the board paid their fair share since she told me that some people do not pay their fair share for over 20 years. She said that why there should be a vote. However no one vote the board, they just seize power. She knows about everything that happened, particularly about the rent hikes. I also sent her everything by emails about the court cases, as well as the president spits on my face when I left court on December 3rd, 2013, part B of the HP action case (trial). I also sent her all the court papers I receive from the board's lawyers electronically, as well as all the papers that the board sent to us. She also knew about the fake Bylaws because I came with the fake Bylaws to her office at the first meeting I had with her, in her office. She also agreed to have the board to kick me out of the apartment. That was what she said loud in the meeting that took place a week before Thanksgiving 2013. Only few shareholders attended to the meeting, particularly all the Haitians and the board's families. The other shareholders did not receive any letter of invitation to attend at the meeting. This meeting was served as fear or threat for the trial of the HP action 2013. I told her that this meeting is pointless and had to do about the HP action case 2013. I was even force by the Board and the lady from UHAB to give fake paper that may turn against me in the future. I have been told not to talk at the meeting if I did not give this fake paper to them, since I happened to be the first one to attend at the meeting. That was a mistake and never let this happened in the next ridiculous and pointless meetings that took place in the future. She is an accessory to what happened to us. Some of the shareholders even blamed her for happened to us on some kind of special the meeting that took place in November 2014. This meeting should have been the end of the board. That never happened. Two lawyers came to talk to the board and found out the problem is worst because they found out that the board never keep records of anything. I knew about that already. No wonder I turned everything that the board did against the board in court. Therefore, the board is still finding ways to stay in charge.

The Super: His name is (omitted). That is the name that the president gives me before I went to court in August 2013. The super is also part of the problem because some shareholders told me that he damaged their properties and never fixed them. I knew about the damaged other shareholders' properties when I talked to them about the damage he had done on the bathroom floor. The board knew about all of the wrong doing and they never did anything about that. He also like to sabotage some shareholders' properties and stated that he found them like that. One of the shareholders told me to watch out for him because that is what he does. However, it was too late for that because I was victimized by him about sabotaging the pipe that was under the bathroom sink and try to make me pay for maintenance. He also said that he had found the pipe under the bathroom sink was already damaged before he removed it. Check the bathroom floor issue for more details. Who knows if the super has qualification and certification to perform certain works in the apartments and the buildings?

The Stock Certificate: I knew of the stock certificate when I have to deal with the bathroom floor situation. The board, particularly the president mentioned it to me when I spoke with him about the bathroom floor issue. He asked if my father had a stock certificate. I said to him that I did not know if my father had one. He told me that it is an obligation for my father to have one because the apartment is there for sale in case my father wants to sell the apartment. My father never told me anything about stock certificate. He also said that my mother and my name must be on the stock certificate. He said that If my father did not have one, he and other board members would issue him one. He also said that how come the CEO/Chair never issued every shareholder stock certificate. I told him that issue my father one, and I would hold it for him. However, the board and their lawyer have been used the stock certificate as a tool to discriminate against me in court. The stock certificate never mentioned in the courtroom, in front of the judges. The lady at the Private sector was also part of that as well. The question that should be asked here is that how many apartments sold in both buildings with the stock certificate, particularly the apartment next to me and above me, since they use to belong to shareholders, as well as other apartments that used to belong to other shareholders in both buildings. Another question should be asked to whom that a shareholder can sell his/ her apartment if the apartment can really sell. It was the president who mentioned about the stock certificate to me first when I talked to him about the damage done by the super on July 16, 2013. He asked me if my father has stock certificate and the stock certificate expires every two years.

Alienation: the board finds that everyone in the buildings are alienated from each other, and uses this as a tool to control the buildings through discrimination, prejudice, hypocrisies, and unfairness. It is the Haitians that the board hated the most in the buildings because they want the Haitians out of the buildings, even though the Haitians do not pose threat and problems to them and anyone else in the buildings. The board tries to raise the rent on the Haitians in January 2013, until one of them found out about that when she spoke with the shareholder who lives in the apartment below me. The shareholder, who lives below me, told her that he did not know anything about the rent hikes in January 2013. The shareholder also told me that she called the gentleman at the Private sector and the lady at the Public sector if they knew about the rent hikes. They said they did not know anything about the rent hikes of January 2013. There was a meeting going on about that, and the meeting did not turn out well. The board's meeting always turned out so bad. No wonder why my father said he never attend to any meetings held by the board because there is nothing serious they would talk about. Even the meeting about the rent hikes postponed two to three times in 2013. There are also other alienations. One of them is that the board, particularly the president, do not like when they see shareholders talk to each other. They did not really want the shareholders to know about their wrongdoings. They like everyone stay away to each other and try their wrongdoings on them individually. The board also went around and said that I lost every court case, the judge ruled over me, which was false. The board also went around and said that I wanted to sue for $ 3000 dollars instead of $ 2000 which is a reimbursement of the money that I spent to rebuild the bathroom floor. My labor came for free during the time I did the work. I have to charge them for my labor, transportation, get rid of the trash now. I was not going to charge them if the board fix the bathroom floor when the problem occurred. They have to bear all the cost of the bathroom floor because they have been very, irresponsible, careless, arrogant, and ignorant to do something about the problem. Another alienation that causes by the board is that they choose who they want to invite in their pointless, ridiculous meetings. The board either drop letters under some shareholders' doors or send letters to some shareholders. They choose whoever to come to their pointless, ridiculous meetings when they know that some of the shareholders really challenging them.

The gentleman at the Public sector: I send all the court papers and some response to the Management at the Public sector because he thought that I came to court verbally and unprepared. He told me that the Judge would never listen to me even though I am right because I do not have a lawyer. I went to see him almost a week after the Marshal came to kick us out of the apartment. He even said to me that the board kicked me out because I did not pay the rent. I showed him proof that I paid the rent, and the rent had been refuse by the board. I decide to send the court papers (HP action and Holdover Proceeding) along with the response I sent to the board's lawyers by mail. I just want him to never Judge a book by its cover. He was the one I talked over the phone when I was in court with the board on the HP action case either in October or in November 2013. He was the one who told me that the physical structure of the apartment is board responsibility. That had been used against the board on the trial of the HP action. However, he was also the one who told that I should fix the damage done by the super on the phone. He was the one I sent response to when he sent the bills of the buildings in June 2014.

The Proprietary Least: The board said that it has been said in the proprietary least that no shareholder relatives, particularly the spouse of the shareholder shall not inherited the property. It has been said also in the Bylaws. If that is the case, some shareholders passed away many years ago, and they relatives are still living in the apartments. Maybe there is a favoritism going here. I send the copy of the proprietary least I found, on the disk. The board also said that it is the Government law that no shareholder's relatives shall inherit the shareholder's apartment. The board and Lady at the Private sector said that the money that has been collected for monthly maintenance is for outside of the buildings.

The TIL: I went to the Private sector's website and found out about the TIL on October 2013. The Lady at the Private sector never said anything about the TIL when I paid her visit twice during the time I was in court. As I said before she agrees with everything that the Board does, even though she knew that what they did all alone is wrong. I send the copy of the TIL on the disk to Authority. The gentleman at the Public sector never said anything about the TIL while on the phone with him during the time of the HP action case. There is a problem with the Proprietary Lease. The Proprietary Lease never included on the TIL. Only the By Laws included.

Research I did about HDFC: during the time I was in court for the HP action cases: I also sent the links of the articles in found out about HDFC, along with their titles. Everything I found that is wrong in some HDFC Co-Ops is also found in the buildings that I live in. The buildings control by the board who thought they are above of everything. The board control by bunch of people who are power hungry. The board control by bunch of people who like to create and make things up, as well as lies. The board control by bunch of people who are taking advantage of other people such as having their children to inherit their places and the buildings. The board lives in their apartments and may not pay their fair shares. The board likes to invade in people's privacy which is illegal to do so. The board like to commit prejudice, arrogant, ignorant, carelessness, unfairness, favoritism, disrespectful, injustice, and discrimination, toward some shareholders, particularly the one that they really do not like.

Meeting: There were only few shareholders that came to the meeting that took place a week and half before thanksgiving. Majority of people or shareholders did not attend to the meeting because they were not welcome to the meeting. One shareholder relative told me that they never knew about the meeting, as well as not receiving any letter for the meeting. As I said to the lady at the Private sector about the meeting was pointless and had to do with the HP-action, which it did. Those who were at the meetings were all the Haitians they tried to raise the rent on, the shareholder below me, the shareholder relative who passed away relative, the manager's mother and one relative, another shareholders who live on the 4th floor. I told the lady at the Private sector that I would attend at the meeting and the Board had some though questions to answer. The letter had two papers. One of them had to do about a "Proxy" paper. I had been pressured to give the proxy paper. I happened to be the first one to show up on time, which I regretted to do so. They told me that I could say anything at all if I did not give the Proxy paper. I did not give any paper. Why should I be a proxy inside my father's apartment? They said if I did not sign the attendance and the attendance for the shareholder, I could not stay. I signed the attendance for shareholder while wrote on it that I represent both of my parents. Everyone started to come around 7: 15pm. The meeting started around that time at the lobby of the building I lived. The meeting lasted about 25 minutes. The lady from UHAB did all of the talking and said things that the board said related to the proprietary least. The lady at the Private sector said in the meeting that not to accept payment from any shareholder's relative who passed away. Ask them for the record for the Proxy paper and for the attendance.

Part 2

Going to Court

W hen my father left the apartment few months after the death of the CEO/Chairman in 2008, not only due to his retirement from his job, but he knew what was going to happen in the buildings which had to do about rent hikes. That was something I found out about on my own. On the day that he left, he went to knock on the head's apartment door, across us at 2B, and told her that we are going to take care of the apartment during his absence. My father showed us, particularly me, how to endorse the money orders and give them to the Head because she was the collector of the money orders. My father also told me that to only buy money orders at the post office, and never explained to me the reason why it is important to only buy money orders there for the apartment. I never knew how my father used to pay for the apartment until on the day he left. My father happened to be one of these type of people who like to keep things to himself, especially when it comes to the problems that surrounding the buildings. He used to say that sometimes that we have no idea what is going on in the buildings. He did not even tell me what HDFC stood for as well. I had zero information about the buildings, but only being alert and vigilant at what I heard and received what has been said to me and given to me.

I was under suspicious that something was not right on the day the fire occurred on February 2006. The board was under pretense by saying to my father that he needed help and never asked for help. The board said that in front of everyone at the lobby; including in front of the firefighters, who put out the fire while they were on their way out of the building. My father ignored the board. The board effectively knew that we never get maintenance at all, as well as all of the problems that happened in the buildings. My father and the board knew that they would never do good work in the apartment after the fire. All the board did in six months after the fire was putting sheetrock across the wall from the Livingroom since the wall wear out all by itself. The board also used cheap paint to paint only the hallway and the living room. They did not do the wall that started to wear out in the bedroom. I ended up spent money to buy sheetrock and paid the same friend which done the work on the bathroom floor for me. He just placed the sheetrock on the actual wall just to give the sheetrock support to hold still and steady. He did the work for me early 2013. I bought paint to paint the hallway, and part the bedroom, which happened to be on the sheetrock I just placed in that same year.

The Livingroom and the hallway had been painted after the fire that occurred on February 2006. The floor remained unclean and undone since it was covered with tiles after the fire. The people who came to do the work after the fire did not clean the floor. Not even the board came to the apartment after the work. I decided to buy hard tiles and placed them on the tiles that had been on the floor, to provide more protection from the leak issues and problems that the apartment suffered from, except the bedroom's floor and bathroom's floor. The bedroom had new tiles on the floor. Another thing my father never told me what kind of building that we live, as well as knowing about the board. I never knew about the difference between living in a building control by Landlord and living in a CO-OP. I also never knew if there were different types of Co-Ops, such as private and public. What about HDFC CO-OP? Does HDFC CO-OP half private and half public? I began to know a lot about Housing issues, situations, and problems while doing research and investigation on my own; during the time I was in court from the HP action case, small claim case, and holdover proceeding case.

I never knew about the Public sector and Private sector, except the lady at the Private sector. The lady at the Private sector gave me her business card one day in 2010 or 2011, after she attended to a meeting that had to do about raising the rent illegally. I came at the end of the meeting which turned into a disaster. No wonder why my father never went to meetings held by the board because the meetings always turned into disaster. The lady at the private sector always there to witness everything that happened in these meetings as I mentioned before. My father used to receive mail from the Private sector and that has been stopped until the Public sector took control over that, or not. I did not know why the changes happened. These letters that used to send to my father had to do about rent reduction. I do not know for how long my father used to receive these letters from the Private sector and Public sector. My father likes to keep things to himself as I mentioned before. These letters sent to my father from the Public sector and Private sector after my father left the apartment. The lady at the Private sector and the gentleman at the Public sector who sent the bill of the buildings knew about all of the illegal rent hikes, as well as the one that happened on 2013 which went up by more than ten percent. The lady at the Private sector witnessed what happened in the meeting and never did anything at all since the buildings are under her watch, or not.

I was not in the meeting that took place on 2013 because I was at work. I heard about the outcome of the meeting from the shareholder who affected by the July 2010 fire and used to stand against the board. Who always behind everything that happened in the buildings was the president. It was the head and the manager allowed the president to do what had been going on in the buildings after the death of the CEO/Chair in May 2008. I always thought that the rent hikes done by the Public sector or Private sector, or other group of people that the tenants of the buildings never knew and saw; and told the board what to do. There are further details about the issues and problems in the buildings about that on part three. No wonder why I did not listen to the board, especially the president after they made me filled out application about the rent reduction and sent it to the Public sector in 2013, during my father's absence. The board knew about my father's absence and they still told me to fill it out by putting my father's name and my mother's name. The president told me not to include my name on the application which made me wonder why I should not. That had become an issue for us until during the time I was in court with board and found out that the board always made decisions without the approval form the shareholders (tenants) and blame these decisions on the shareholders. No wonder why the Private sector and Public sector may get affected by the wrongdoings done by the board.

After the super damaged the bathroom floor I leveled and built on July 2, 2013, the board knew about it and never did anything despite the facts that I wanted to collaborate with them by buying materials to have the board fix the bathroom floor. Therefore, the board decided to let their arrogance, ignorance, and stupidity got the best of them. I still do the best I could to work things out with the board even though they imposed accusation on me over the bathroom's floor, as well as given me fake Bylaws. When I found out that the board remained irresponsible, careless, arrogant and ignorant about the damage done on the bathroom's floor, I decided to go to court. Before I went to court, as well as not knowing which court I had to go to, I decided to do research online about finding a lawyer for my case. I also started to write about the bathroom floor issues and problem. I also started to do some secret recordings on my own because of what the president said to me on July 16, 2013, which had pushed me to do some secret recordings. The first recording was to face the super on July 17, 2013 at 9:00am and told him about what the president said. I moved from one lie to another. The second recording I did was on the president. What the president said on the second recording when I asked him about the Bylaws, the Stock Certificate, the full name of the super, and everyone's full names in charge. The president said that he would get the Bylaws and it would take times because the Bylaws is forty pages. The president also said my father should be the one to add me on the stock certificate and wanted to collect the stock certificate from my father had in order to give him a new Stock Certificate.

The president added just because we pay for my father that does not mean we can stay in the apartment. The president also said that it was him and the others allowed us to stay. He gave the super's full name since that was the first thing I asked him. I did not even know the super's name until that day. Speaking of knowing few names in the buildings was not the subject of my interest. Only my brother knew few names in the buildings. I received the Bylaws few days later and read. I receive the Bylaws along with the list names of the people in charge, with their phone numbers included. The top of the paper said "board member information" without any address of HDFC in it, as well as the names of the board of directors. I wondered why they did not include their addresses on the paper. The copy of that paper sent to Authority, along with the fake Bylaws. These documents would not include in the book. I made research on the internet and found information about one law firm among others. I decided to call the law firm. The person I talked on the phone told me that it would cost me ten thousand dollars to have a lawyer to take the bathroom case, after I explained to him about the damage done by the super, and the people in charge did not do anything about it. It was kind of very costly to pay a lawyer for the damage, especially without seeing the damage first. I was wondering how much it would have costed me for the other problems that the bathroom suffered, as well as the whole problems in the apartment and took on all problems that occurred in the buildings.

The person I spoke to on the phone told me that the only option I had was to go to the Civil Court that located in downtown Brooklyn. The person gave me the address of the Civil Court in downtown Brooklyn. I made another search on the internet and found information about the Civil Court. I made a phone call. I explained the issues and problems to the person work at the court and he told me to come to file for small claim. However, things were not the way I imagined them to be when I came to court. There were few things I had to deal with while was in court. One of them was the Judge told me to go on the fourth floor to get advice from lawyer after spending hours sitting in the courtroom. When I got on the fourth floor and met with a lawyer who worked for the court, in her office. The lawyer told me that she was unable to represent me because I am not the tenant of the apartment, even though it was my father's. The lawyer said the only way she could represent me only if my father signed paper which proven that my father passed his tenancy's right to me. I told the lawyer that my father is absent at this moment and went to Haiti. The lawyer said tried to send the paper works to Haiti electronically to have my father sign and send the paper back to me. How in the hell I would be able to do that? Where this paper work should be coming from? The board knew about my father's absence. Was it the board responsibility to make the paper works happened, before my father left?

My father said to me that do not do anything under his name before he left. Everything the lawyer said to me sound so strange because they made me wonder if there is a law saying that a child cannot represent his/her parent in court. I left the lawyer's office and came back about half hour later in the same place to speak with the lawyer who was actually there given advice to people who came to court; without knowing or had no knowledge of what was going on in court. While the lawyer talked to me, I did not mention anything about my father at all to him. The court cases I wrote about had a lot of details about what the lawyer said was different than what another lawyer said to me almost one month later. The other lawyer did not work for the court. The other lawyer gave me advice not to become a lawyer because it is a nasty business, after I spoke with him about my situation. He also added that one learned a lot when you come to court.

He was right about, unless one wanted to learn quickly. However, both lawyers never asked me about what type of CO-OP I lived in. Therefore, they ended up given me different kind of answers about CO-OP buildings. There will be more details about what they said to me in few of the report I sent to Authority. After I took all of the advices and information; I decide to forge a letter and signed it under my father's name to go to court with. I wrote exactly what he said verbally to the head that lived across us on the day he left, that my mother and I would pay under his name during his absence. The court always crowed with people during the time filed the court cases and being in the courtroom. I began to see that housing issues and problems in Brooklyn is a very serious matter. You can literary hear people cases because they are right in the open for anyone in the courtroom to hear them unless if it was a trial. The trial usually happened in private because the trial is a crucial part of the case, or any court cases.

I met with my uncle when I came to court after I file for the second HP action case on the hallway. I found surprise of him, telling me that he had rats coming in his apartment. His apartment looked better than our apartment. He lived across the street from the Botanic garden in Brooklyn. He did not pay so that they can come to fix the apartment. He showed me the money orders. It seemed to me he spent probably one year or two not paying because the money orders were a lot. He told me they will never come to make repairs when I paid the rent every month because all they need is the money. He said that he kept the payment of the rent until they brought him to court to prove the reason why he did not pay. However we were not in the same courtroom for our cases. He also told me that raising the rent on people who had been living in their apartments for twenty years or more should not happen. He added that they just wanted to force people out of the buildings. He wanted to make sure that this never happened to him. He was surprised about what we had to go through after the illegal eviction took place probably in a year and a half later over the phone. He told me to be careful with the people in my buildings because they can murder me for that. He even added that I should sent letter to Washington DC about my problem because the court may not be able to do anything about my case, over the complexities that surrounded it.

Let see what happened within the HP action cases that kept as personal record. I did the best I could to get some of what happened in court and kept them as my personal record. I was lucky I did that not only for the HP action case, but the small claim case, and the holdover proceeding case. I also kept record of what was going on outside of the court as well in court because they were very important. There were three things I found out that some lawyers did in court, particularly when these lawyers playing dirty games. The first thing is being unpredictable. The second thing is some lawyers have intention to change what they do and say when there is more than one Judge handling a court case. The third thing some lawyers do is to create confusion. There is one more thing I want to say before I provide details about these three things. I want to say that never go to court empty handed. All of these three things happened at once in all of the court cases I had been with the board and their lawyer(s). Another thing I found in court was that being a petitioner or defendant may go vice versa because you can be a petition who puts on defensive mode, as well as being a defendant who puts on petition mode. Can a defendant become a witness? That was what happened during the trial of the holdover proceeding. That may never happened at all in any court cases. If it does, the percentage may be lower.

I have been experienced both of being petitioner and defendant during my time in court. Despite all of these three things going on in court, the Judges knew about them and being very careful and alert about them when they appear in court. Being in court facing the Judges is like prisoner dilemma to some degree. There are three types of unpredictability that the board and their lawyer(s) committed on the HP action case. the first unpredictability that the board and their lawyers provided was when they accused me by saying that I want to sue HDFC, that was why I did not have inspector to come in the apartment, as well as I am not the shareholder. The board's lawyer said that aloud and tried to embarrass me in front of everyone who was in the courtroom that day. The board (president) and the lawyer were laughing and smirking about what they said as if they were having fun with it. I responded to the Judge about the bathroom issue by saying that I spent over nine hundred dollars to build it and it was damage by the super. I pointed my finger to the president and said that the president knew about it. I asked the Judge what does he wants me to do about it and who is going to pay for the damage. The Judge responded by saying that he cannot tell me what to do; I should figure it out. The Judge added by saying that to give him five minutes, he would give me something. He gave me copy of what he wrote, and gave the same copy to the board and the board's lawyer. The copy of the paper is not included in the book as well.

It was the Judge who trapped the board and the board's lawyer because the Judge did not know about the bathroom floor issues and problems. It was what the Judge wrote on paper made me to confess, as well as report about everything. It was the same Judge who gave order on the second HP action case that I filed when I came back to court few days later. The second unpredictability that the board and the board's lawyer committed was when I came to court on the second HP action. The board and their lawyer ignored the response I sent to them and tried to come up with something else as a backup strategy. The board and their lawyer gave me a paper to read before I faced the judge. Therefore, that was evident that they ignore what I sent to them and tried to do something else. That also counted as a big foul for the board and the board's lawyer. I played by the rules of the court based on what the first Judge of the second HP action told me what I must do. I saw a different Judge when I came back to court after inspector came to the apartment. I contradicted what the board said in court because that was what they reported to the court as ridiculous case against me and brought them on trial.

The third unpredictability that the board committed on the day of the trial was to change lawyer and trying to bring me back where I left off with them. They tried to change what they did and said before the trial. I moved forward with everything while the board was moving backward. I could not give anything to the Judge after the Judge found the board guilty. The Judge could have collected what I bought in court, the day I brought the board on trial because the Judge knew about the response I sent to the board's lawyer, despite the fact that the lawyer lied in front of the Judge. The Judge could have prevented the board from changing lawyer. I had no idea why the Judge let things happened this way. Maybe each and every Judge has different strategy and tactic to deal with what happened or went on in the courtroom. I found out what happened on the trial of the HP action as a waste of my time, and the court should be held responsible and accountable for the outcome of the trial. The board and the board's lawyer knew what they did. The board and their lawyer did whatever it took to prevent the response I sent to their lawyer, as well as what their lawyer sent to me by mail, to go to the Judge. No wonder why the board's lawyer tried to force the Judge to close the case before he lied and contradicted what he and his clients done (the board) before I brought them on trial. The lawyer even scared off the lady who brought the court case file to the Judge by smacking his fingers in front of the Judge and printed one index finger on her to stay away. As for my part I was partially confused about such behavior. As for the president, he pretended that he was not part of anything, but only there to help the head. The president got involved when I pulled out the Bylaws.

The second thing that the board and the board's lawyer did was to change what they said and did when there are more than one Judges handling the same case. When the board and the board's lawyer found out they would trap with something, they would do what it takes to change that and pretend that it never happens. No wonder I never let that happened in all of my court cases when I discovered what the board and their lawyer(s) had been doing. It was also crucial move for the board and their lawyer(s), as well as anyone to make because the court would effectively know about it unless the party suffers from it, brings it to the court's attention.

The third thing that the board and their lawyer did was to commit confusion at what they were doing in court. The board and their lawyer committed not only confusion at what they did in court, but also committed confusion to me when I came to court. That happened because what the board and their lawyer sent to me was different than what they said and did in court before and/or after I received the papers that they sent to me by mails. I had to see through what the board and their lawyer doing in order to get myself out of the confusion that the board and their lawyer created. The board and their lawyer created confusion in order to be unclear about what they did and had the court case close, discontinued, or dismiss. However, the court would always have everything playing out in the courtroom to see how far the court case would go. I would never be able to bring the board on trial if I did not aware, as well as discover what the board and their lawyer had been doing. The HP action could have been closed, dismissed, or discontinued without a trial if I did not do anything at all about it. Who knows how many lawyers out there; operating the same manner just like, the board's lawyer(s) do in the housing court on a daily basis? What the board and their lawyer(s) did in the courtroom and out of the courtroom were messy, dirty, and ugly. The outcomes of the HP action cases along with the copies of documents that I received in court from the Judges are included on part two. These documents and the outcome of the HP action cases sent to Authority. The documents had been sent to the gentleman at the Public sector and the lady at the Private sector.

• Send to Authority on January 2014

The outcome of the HP action cases
Compare and contrast the HP action cases

The outcome of the First HP action: Index Number (omit)

When I went to court on July 31, 2013, to have the HP action done, I went for only the bathroom floor issue. I was lucky that I have almost everything in writing about the bathroom floor issue and went to court with it. I add on it when I heard different from the lawyer who gave me advised. I did not have inspector to come in the apartment due to the reason that who is going to pay for the damage. I also have the letter that the board sent to some shareholders whom they thought who could not read, which indicated not to have inspector comes to the shareholders apartment if they feel uncomfortable with that. I also did not know if the board took lawyer. The board lawyer said that I did not want inspector to come in the apartment because I wanted to sue HDFC, as well as I am not the shareholder. The judge asked me who I am, and if I went on trial, I would lose. I asked the Judge who is going to pay for the damage done by the super on the bathroom floor that I built in May 2012. I pointed my finger on the president by saying that he knew about the bathroom floor issue. I asked the Judge what he wanted me to do about that. The Judge said he cannot tell me what to do, but I should figure it out. I said to the judge if that is what the board wanted, I would find other problems in the apartment because they are there. The judge helped me to withdraw from the HP action case, and told me that to give him 5 minutes because he would give me something. He wrote a note on paper and gave me a copy, and gave the president a copy as well. The president's lawyer asked the judge how he was going to pay. The judge told him to read the paper (with anger in his face). Since the board said I wanted to sue HDFC, I did a lot of research about HDFC and find much more that can use against the board, such as discrimination, prejudice, suspicious of fraud, and many more problems. The Judge stated on his decision that the board (defendant) must paid for the lawyer's fees. The board ended up charge my father for the lawyer fees by added to the August 2013 receipt.

The outcome of the second HP action: Index Number (omit)

I had the second HP action done the second time and had inspector came in the apartment. On the day I went to court to have the HP action done, I spoke with a lawyer around the hallway about the issue. He asked me if my father and I share the responsibilities. I said yes, we share the responsibilities. He said that the rent money that you pay every month is the maintenance. I began to see something is wrong there because the board said that the maintenance everyone paid for the buildings go directly to fix pipes and the buildings themselves. Maintenance has been paid for more than 27 years and the buildings look like trash. The buildings have been painting twice since I lived in it. The paint has been used to cover problems. I went back to court on August 29, 2013 to see the first judge for the second HP action. I showed the judge, the picture of the bathroom floor, and the judge was surprised by what she saw. I let her knew that damage done by the super, as well let her knew that I am the son of the shareholder, and I have been living in the apartment since 1996. I let the judge knew that the wife of the shareholder is living in the apartment, since the board excluded her from everything. I even showed the judge the paper that the first judge gave me on the first HP action, as well as the lawyer charges that the president and the board want us to pay for. They charged me under my father's name and claimed that the Bylaws and proprietary least says so. The judge said to me that the HP action does not give money. I said to the judge that no problem, I already have it done. I showed her the paper I wrote about the bathroom floor issues. The judge told me that the board's lawyer is going to send me something, and I have the right to disagree. I said to the judge no problem. The lawyer sent me almost the same thing that he had the first HP action. I even talked to him on day I came to court, to tell him I read his paper and it full with lies, before I saw the judge. He did not say anything. I received both papers one day after I left court. The first one was delivered to me through the head" son by knocking on my door. The second one was delivered under my door, and not knowing who delivered it. Both papers came from on head's apartment, and I had the suspicion that she tried to frame me with her apartment. I sent my response to the lawyer along with a proposal, the outcome of the inspection, and the bathroom floor issue. I have to let you know that the board started to hide other problems in the buildings on the next day when the president left court on September 2013. These problems are paintings, boilers, hiding cracks that had been around for so many years, and fixing windows that had been damaged for so many years. The board even lied about the boilers had been damaged in 2009, so that they could raise the rent. I have them recorded and sent them along with everything else. Some of the people who came to do work in front of the building told me miraculously that the board is not doing good work at all in front of the buildings. I let them know that are not doing good work at all in most of the apartments. The board used the super to paint inside the buildings, as well as hiding the cracks.

When I came back to court on October 17, 2013, the board lawyer called out my name and gave me a paper about 5 to 10 minutes before I saw the judge. I read the paper and I laugh. I also did not know what they report to the judge. The judge told me that if the board fixes the apartment, the board would charge my father for it because the apartment is there for sale. I said to judge that we are not going to sell anything. I said to the judge that I have the Bylaws, show me my responsibility. I showed the judge the picture of the damage on the ceiling in the living room, that has been there for six years and ignore by the board, particularly the head. She knew about the problem and never did anything about it. I pointed my finger on her and said to the judge she knew about it. I said to the judge I sent something to the board's lawyer, and he lied in front of the judge that he did not received anything. I showed the judge the copy of what I sent to the board's lawyer. The judge looked at it. I said to the judge that there are some contradictions at what the board's lawyer sent me, as well as gave the board a proposal. I said to the judge that I get advice from a lawyer and told me what my responsibilities are. I said to the judge that I would do 30% and the board had to do 70%. I also said to the judge to go back to the fire that happened in year 2005 or 2006. The board yelled no. I told the judge that I would buy materials to put on the floor and the board must be paid for labor. The judge said to come back with everything I had for part B (trial) on December 3rd, 2013. I received the third of the same paper that the board lawyer gave to me in court, sitting in the mail box after I left court on October 17, 2013 late on the afternoon. He made the correction on the apartment number, as well as received my response.

When I came back to court on December 3rd, 2013, I saw the board smiling. I wondered why they were smiling. When they saw that they were about to see the same judge for part B, they were surprised. I also did not know if the board switched lawyer for part B. I asked the court officer is that allowed for the defendant to change lawyer. The court officer said yes, it is allowed. I could hear them outside of the courtroom talked to their lawyer about I am not the shareholder of the apartment. When the board's lawyer represent that to court, the judge said that is totally unrelated to the court cases, and I am in court helping my father, there is nothing wrong with that. I let the judge knew that the board composed of people who are the board of directors, the board, and shareholders. I let the judge knew that I called somebody at the Public sector and the person told me that the board is responsible for the physical structure of the apartment, not the shareholder. I let the judge knew that fiduciary responsibility of the board is to take care of their shareholders. I let the judge knew that the apartment suffered from mice and roaches. The board claimed that they sent people to fix the apartment. I said they sent the super to check on the smoke detector. The board said that my apartment is 100% woods. I said to the judge that the floor covered with tiles, and no one asked me what kind of tiles the floor covered with. The board showed the paper that the first judge gave me on the first HP action to their lawyer and the judge. I did not know what they tried to do with it. I let the judge knew that the bathroom has been damaged by the super that I built on May 2013. The board came with the Bylaws or Proprietary least. I showed to the judge the picture of the bathroom floor and the board's lawyer. I came with some of the HP actions letters (serve the board) that I sent to the board and some of them returned to me. The first one on the HP action had the green cards on the front of the envelopes when I had the first HP action done. I did not put the green cards on the front of the envelopes for the second HP action. I also did not know if that is a big deal or not to the court. I did not include the green cards due to the reason that it cost me more money. The board lawyer and the judge said they would send an inspector to check the apartment. I said sure it is fine with me, sent the inspector. I told them who is going to fix the damage when they remove the tiles I have on the floor. They board's lawyer said I would fix it myself. I said; do not send anyone in that case.

When the judge told the board and their new lawyer to go and come later on, the board still persistent with the proprietary least. I told the board's lawyer I have a proprietary least, let compare and contrast them. I also let the judge and the lawyer know to ask the board about how many pages the Bylaws is. I persist at the end by saying that what the board had is the Bylaws. The judge said lets go on trial. When I took seat and the judge told me raising my right hand to swear what I said is true. I said I do. The judge told me that the case is mine, and the judge said she does not have enough time for a lot, but show her what I have. I had a lot to show, but I did not get any specification from the judge about what I need to show in court. I said to the judge I withdraw from the case, and said to the board they must pay for their lawyer. The President cursed at the Judge. When I was in the hallways, I said to the president whatever he and the others are doing is illegal. I asked him if he has a job. He walked aggressively toward me and spat on my face. I spat back on his face. One of the court officers heard everything and came out. She told me to leave because both of us should have been arrested. She told me it is Ok, and that happened in court very often, and aware what is going on. My next move is the small claim. They tried to get themselves out of that by using the same strategy not being the one in charge. The judge said to proceed with the case on April 10, 2014. No wonder why the lawyer who gave me advice said that the HP action is quicker than the Small Claim, as well as telling whoever is in charge of a building would be held responsible and accountable for the super's mess. One thing that I forgot to mention was that the Judge blamed me when she found out that I made repairs on the bathroom floor with my money.

Note: sent to Authority

Letter sent to the lady at the Private sector

Actual date of the letter 8/9/2013

Dear (name omitted)

My name is (omitted) and I send you this letter on the behalf of my father, (name omitted), who is the shareholder of the apartment. My father has been retired from work and let me and my mother responsible of the apartment. He does not put it on paper, but let the board in the building knew about that. He verbally said to the head, a board member that my mother and I would be in charge of the apartment. I also put it in writing for him and made him sign it before he left, along with date he signed it. I do not know anything about transferring of name to name to take responsibility of the apartment. I also do not know other complications that come along with that until I have to deal with the bathroom floor's problem that occurred on July 2, 2013. I have more details about that on a letter I should have sent to the civil court. The letter is after this part. I also find it so strange that we spent more than $100,000 in 32 years for the apartment that has been damaged since the day my father and us have moved in, yet nothing has been done about that, as well as internal problems that the apartment suffers from. We just keep patch things in the apartment up till now. I went to court on August 9, 2013 just to get the money I spent to build the floor last May 2012. The super damaged the bathroom floor and the board does not want to take responsibility about that. The board gets lawyer because they think I want to sue them for money. I withdraw from everything and start over. However on the day I went to the civil court (7/31/2013), I talked to a civil service lawyer about the issue that occurred on July 2, 2013. The lawyer told me that it does not matter about the damage done by the super; it is the landlord who is responsible for that. He told me to go get the HP action done. I do the HP action without have inspection come to the apartment; I just want the board in the building pays for the damage that the super caused on the floor I built last May 2012 with the money I spent on. I spent $ 950 dollars to build the floor last May 2012. I have to let you know that I have no intention of suing anybody for that, including HDFC and the Private sector. The board in the building is being control by bunch of people who happen to be arrogant, ignorant, negligent, careless, and irresponsible. I have more detail on the letter I should have send to the Civil Court in writing. I need your help to see how these issues can be handling without my father's presence. I heard from other lawyers that it could be a problem for me if I want to deal with the problem due to the fact that I am not the shareholder. However I am the son of the shareholder. We keep paying the apartment under his name after he left in 2008. I also want to know where I could find help for rent increases because the president says to me that he can increase the rent any time after the government no longer be part of anything next June 2014. We have been against the rent hikes that the board members in the building done many time in the past. One more thing, we cannot be held responsible for any other problems that occur in the building financially because we pay our rent on time and never owe rent, as well as pay rent late. I am looking forward to hear from you. I also want you to know that I take the board in the building to court now due to unfair treatment. I have HP action done this week (7/13/2013) as well as small claim of $ 2000 dollars from the head due to damage of property and other claims (7/12/2013). I have to be in court with her on December 19, 2013. I also want to know if the board members (names omitted) raise the rent on themselves as well. I have been trying to reason to them, they have been too stubborn.

Sincerely

Name omitted

Address omitted

Email address omitted

Phone number omitted

Part 3

Troubles

There were three types of troubles that I discovered while being outside of the courtroom during the HP Action cases. These three types of trouble were anonymous, research, and investigation. I have to say that it was the board and their lawyer(s) who brought these troubles to themselves. The board and their lawyer(s) played the same game of staying anonymous. They both had been playing anonymous not only on the HP action cases, but also in the small claim case and on holdover proceeding case. The three envelops that the board's lawyer(s) sent to me had three problems. The first problem was that there were no names included on each envelop that the board's lawyer(s) sent to me. Each envelop also sent to me on the eve of the court dates, which also a problem. Each court case in each envelop did not have the dates of the cases the board's lawyer(s) sent to me. It seemed to be that the board's lawyer(s) prepared these cases probably in few days or few weeks before getting closer to the court dates. The first two envelops sent by law firm known as G***** and L*** PLLC. Each case from the two envelops sent by G***** and L*** PLLC and these envelops sent to the wrong apartment (2B). However, there was something strange and weird went on about the third envelop; after I sent response to G***** and L*** PLLC. The third envelop sent by G***** and L***LLP, and the case was prepared by G***** and L*** PLLC. There was no name on the third envelop as well.

No wonder why the first lawyer came to court playing nasty and dirty game before I brought the HP action case on trial. The law firm of G***** and L*** PLLC and LLP were from the same address. It seemed to be that G***** and L*** PLLC is operated under LLP. That is kind of weird and strange to have a law firm operating inside or within another law firm on the same address. Based on what had been going on was that G***** and L*** PLLC showed up in court first and got stuck with the court case; then G***** and L*** LLP had been used as back up trying to cover the problem that PLLC faced, which done so by and under pretense. No wonder why there was a different lawyer showed up on the trial of the HP action case. I did not remember what the lawyer said about whether or not he recognized the first lawyer, as well as said if he came from G***** and L*** PLLC or LLP. He just said that he replaced the first lawyer. Even the first lawyer never said if he came from G***** and L*** PLLC or LLP as well.

There were three reasons contributed to the replacement of lawyers. The first reason was that G***** and L*** PLLC sent the first two envelops not only on the wrong apartment but also using my first name as my last name, and my last name as my first name. I also receive the first two letters almost two days after I left court. I sent response to G***** and L*** PLLC on the first two cases they sent to me; which caused serious problem to G***** and L*** PLLC and the board. The third envelop sent to the right apartment, but with my last name used as first name, and my first name used as last name. Another problem that included on the third envelop sent by G***** and L*** LLP was that they included my father into the situation, and misspelled my father's first name on purpose. The board and their lawyer(s) started to change things that also affected what happened on the small claim case. The board and their lawyer(s) used what they sent to me on the third envelop to use for the holdover proceeding case. I did not write my father's name on the response that I sent to G***** and L*** PLLC on the HP action case since my father was not in the apartment, as well as my father said not to do anything under his name as I mentioned before. The reason why I mentioned my father on the response that I sent to G***** and L*** PLLC, without writing his full name, was that the board and their lawyer came to court on the first HP action case and said that I was not the shareholder. I did not say anything to the Judge when he asked me who I was. I did not know whether or not that was the case. I was also caught off guard because it was so unpredictable and unexpected that the board came to court to do that to me. It was from the third envelop that the board and their lawyer(s) sent to me resulted to the identity theft, perjury, and falsify information and documents.

All of the three envelops that the board and their lawyer(s) sent to me not only counted as anonymous, but also counted as suspicious envelops. There was something really wrong and strange about the way I received the first two envelops. The first envelop was given to me by the head's son who lived across me at apartment 2B by knocking on my door. The second envelop was pushing under the apartment at 2D. I can barely pushing two to three pages of papers under my apartment's door because the spot under the door was tight. How can the board or whoever had the ability and capability to push a yellow envelop that had about more than six pages of nonsense under the apartment door?

The board also committed anonymous of their own. The very first anonymous was right under my nose. That anonymous was on the receipts that the board gave to everyone after making payments for their apartments. The address that the board putted on the receipts was a trap of its own for two reasons. The first reason was that if one uses the address that on the receipt to send a letter, that letter would come back to that person as "unable to forward". I tried that and knew for fact that it was not going to work. I tried that during the time I was in court on the HP action case, and used it as case against the board. The second reason was that the board used the same address to send envelops to us after the board called police on us on January 3, 2014. The board wanted us to go to the post office to get that envelop which turned out to have my father with his first name misspelling on purpose, at specific time. The people who work at the post office was not going to give it to me because it should be my father who should come to get that envelop, despite the fact that our names included on the envelop. The people who worked at the post office told me that a lot of money had been spent for that envelop, as well said it was a government business. I did check that at the USPS post office website when the card came to my father's name along with the confirmation number.

I was not going to receive that envelop until the manager who worked at the post office made the decision to give it to me. I did not know if I was going to waste my time because that envelop would have sent to receiver instead of sending it back to the sender; and still count as "unable to forward". I found out about that from another envelop that I received from the board as "unable to forward", the same day after I went to pick up the one at the post office. The second envelop was either delivered by one of the postal employee or found it on the mail box. The board never putted their names and their addresses on these envelops. The board did not even put their names and sign the letters that they sent to us on these envelops. The board never put their addresses on these envelops because they knew effectively that they live in their apartments without reported that they live in these apartments. No wonder why I got their full names and knew where they live to go to court with, was the right thing to do for one reason. That reason had to do about what the board told me behind closed door before I went to court was not true. I was under suspicious that it was not true. I used their names and their addresses to file for the HP action.

That also used against the board because I sent six envelops to them. Three envelops from the first HP action and three from the second HP action. One envelop from the first HP action sent back to me as returning mail, which happened to be the head. Two envelops sent back to me on the second HP action case which happened to be the president and the manager. Therefore, that had been proved effectively that the board said they did not live in their apartments. The lady at the private sector knew about these envelops on the second meeting that I had with her for few minutes and decided to kick me out of her office. It was the lady at the Private sector who told me to bring these envelops in court with me when she found that she was trapped with, at what the board had been doing. The Public sector also traps with the board because the Public sector allowed the board to provide them with false information and documents about us and the buildings. People might get fire at the Public sector due to all of these problems that the board created. The Private sector may be in serious trouble because they let the board did whatever they want to do.

I found it so ironic that it was the board and their lawyer, particularly the president, since he was the only one showed up in court on the first HP action case. It was the president and his lawyer gave clues, as well as gave me way out of everything after accusing me of trying to sue HDCF because HDFC was a non-profit organization. I went on the internet to find information about HDFC. I could not believe of all of the articles that I found from the HDFC website. A lot of what I found from some of these articles was effectively used against the board and their lawyer(s). I had to read these articles twice. I had to read them the second time along with the notes I wrote about them. I also read the articles the second time during the time I was near the trial of the HP action case. Some of the articles explained the reason why the board should be rejected. One of these reasons had to about the board control by bunch of prejudice and power hungry individuals. Another reason had to do about the board made up of people who do thing for their families while excluding other families. Another reason had to do about the board created their rules which led to serious problems and troubles for the board. That was what happened in the buildings because the board created their own rules, and claimed that some of these rules happened to be government rules and HDFC rules. No wonder why they tried to raise the rent in a month before the board and their lawyer(s) evicted us illegally, and claimed that it was the government required them to raise the rent. The board moved from the shareholders who made decision to raise the rent on themselves to it was the government which raises the rent on everyone. No wonder I asked the lady at the Private sector that I needed letter sent by the government, along with name and signature on that letter. I also found out that it is only the court, the Supreme Court, which can take away the board's power, or gets rid of the board, when the court finds out that the board has been taken their powers for granted.

One of the articles mentioned about who the board does not allow to be in meetings held by the board. The board decided who should or should not come to the meeting. I have been facing about that toward the board from the HP action case, small claim case, to the holdover proceeding case. The board did not even invite me on the meeting that took place a day after I left court and came back for the trial of the holdover proceeding. Other meetings I had been attended held by the board were useless, bogus and waste of everyone's time because these meeting were like cover ups at what had been going on HP action case, Small claim case, and holdover proceeding case. The board knew effectively that they trapped with everything. The board just made fool out of themselves. Therefore, they ended up made everyone else wasted their time. The board tried to cover all of the problems surrounding the buildings. Therefore, the board ended up makes things worse for themselves.

Another reason had to do about the board use the finances of the buildings for private gain. That was true to what had been going on in the buildings I lived in because the board is effectively used the finance of the buildings for private gain. The article added that it was the shareholders' responsibility to prevent the board from using the buildings' finance for private gain. Where did some of the board' members found money to pay for their cars and their children's cars and other expenses? The article added that the board even wanted their children to inherit them. That also had been going on in the buildings I live in. The board, particularly the president, wanted his wife and children to benefit on the buildings' finance. I discovered online that he included his whole family on the finance of the buildings, in the middle of the year 2016. I did not know if that information was out there to public. I wish I could have known about that and brought it in court on the trial of the holdover proceeding case as evidence and exhibit. The shareholders in the buildings never do anything about the board had been used the buildings' finance as private gain. As for the other board members (the manager and the head), they did theirs in hidings.

Another reason had to do about some of the apartments in the buildings had the floor covered with tiles, while others had woods. That also happened in the building(s) I lived in. The few of the apartments that had woods happened to be the board and their relatives who lived in them. Therefore, the board ended up living other apartment remained into ruined. Another reason had to do about the board like to invade on the tenant's privacy. That was what the board did to me while in court. The board invaded on my privacy and it was effectively used against them. The board even invaded so deep in our privacy where the board intended to steal the apartment from my father's name under identity theft, perjury, and falsify information and documents. One of the kind of prejudice also appeared to the invasion of privacy was income. One of the articles stated that income guideline gave the board ways to commit prejudice toward applicants who try to get apartments at HDFC buildings. The problem that can be caused was that the board would never follow the income guideline that HDFC sets forth. The board would rather create their own income guideline in secret, or rented some of the apartments in the buildings under subletting. The board in the buildings did not want any tenants making less than thirty thousand dollars a year to live in the apartments. Therefore, the board effectively did not follow the income guideline of that of the HDFC set forth.

I found it ironic to some degree about the income issues. The board may **compose** of people who may or may not have incomes of their own, and never pay anything for over twenty years. Therefore, they ended up being freeloaders, as well as behaving like economic gangsters and mafia. One of the articles stated about the fiduciary responsibility of the board was to take care of the shareholders. If the fiduciary responsibility of the board was not met, that was effectively a problem for the board. That fiduciary responsibility issues had been used against the board during the trial of the HP action case. I also added that by saying to the judge that it was a bunch of families taken advantage of other families. It was also wrong of the board to behave like landlord, which went against the rules and regulations of HDFC Co-Ops, as well as subletting and illegal sales of apartments. One of the articles also mentioned about that housing is a big scam and if anyone had been discovered committing scams, a big lawsuit would be against that person. Anyone who made up of the board would never take responsibility of the lawsuit. That was what happened in the buildings I lived in. The board blaming each other, particularly the president, who was blamed more for everything that had been going on. There were few major problems that contributed to the lawsuit in the building I lived in. The scam was not the only one. The identity theft, perjury, and falsify information and documents that the board committed against us which also led to the illegal eviction after the board and their lawyer(s) went against the Judge's decision. The board also rented the apartment under my father's name by removing the marshal notice from the door, under subletting. My mother and I ended up being homeless with nowhere to go, on the day that we were forced out of the apartment. That also caused mental and physical shock and trauma to us, particularly my mother, who was unable and vulnerable to deal with the problem. That illegal eviction had caused me losing my dignity as a human being because I was forced out of the apartment like an animal. What happened to us also contributed to lawsuit against the Co-Op. Above all the board considered to be control by a bunch of criminals. The Public sector and the Private sector contributed as well as accessory to what the board had been doing, particularly the Private sector.

"I did what I could on my own to fill out for apartment on both public and private sector, particularly more in private sector, a week after the illegal eviction. I was allegeable to get an apartment after I have been told that I won the lottery. When my mother and I came for an interview in May 2016, I was under suspicious that the people in the place were trying to disqualify us unfairly. The people in there did what they could, even if they had to go against their own rules, on the day of the interview. I did what I could to remain alert and vigilant. I even stopped them when they asked me something to which never included on the list that they sent to me by email. I also stopped them when they asked me for the Proprietary Lease of the building I lived in, as well as the

record of the rent I paid. I gave them the copies of the Judge's decision on the holdover proceeding case, along with my response collected in court before and during the trial of the holdover proceeding. I received a letter from them in a month late which stated that they found me ineligible to receive the apartment because I made over Twenty nine thousand dollars a year. I did not know where they came to that stupid conclusion. That conclusion would turn against them without having any proof of it. I knew for facts that these people would come up with something in order not to give me the apartment. These people's behavior toward my mother and I was strange and weird. What these people did which would effectively turned against them was that they did exactly what the board and their lawyer did, playing anonymous. The envelope that they sent to me did not have name on it, as well as no name and signature of who made the decision to disqualify me. They were shocked when I sent response to them and told them about these problems. I let them know that they either to bring me in court or I would sent everything to the Justice Department. The person that was interviewed me sent response by email since I told them to, and told me to do an appeal. He did not even tell me where to go to make the appeal, and who should made the appeal. It seemed to be that these people ignored what I sent to them, and tried to do their own things. I specifically told them that I would not waste time to come to their office, but need to move in to the apartment. Therefore, I decided to send my case against them to the Justice Department. What happened to us seemed to be based on prejudice, discrimination, and injustice. Who knows how many people went through what I had been in the City on a daily basis, about unfair and wrongful disqualification for apartments. Despite the fact that these people invaded in our privacy by asking me almost twenty pages of documents, such as six months of bank statements for me and my mother, four months of work pay stubs for me, 2015 income tax for me, and social security retirement letter for my mother. Another problem that the place may face was that it was unclear whether it was an agency, Co-Op (public or private), or landlord. I began to find out that prejudice on housing does not happen in HDFC Co-Ops only. Prejudice happens on housing in general, along with discrimination and injustice to some degree."

It was also illegal of the board to do anything under my father's name while my father was absent. Another lawsuit would be about the CEO/ Chairman's name, had been used as current information while she passed away since May 2008. It was my mother who made me discovered about that miraculously. I found out the CEO/Chairman's name was still in used a day later when I brought the board on trial of the HP action case. It was my mother who told me to go to get help from one of the local government's office located on (address omitted). The person I saw at the office that day, checked information about the buildings on the internet and found who happened to be in charge of the buildings, which was the CEO/Chairman that passed away. I was shocked and could not believe what he found. I thought my eyes were playing tricks on me. I told him to send the link to my email address. We even went to place where the Haitian councilman located on (address omitted). He was there and did not really got help from him and anyone else, and made me wondered why. All me and my mother received from the Haitian lady who talked to us on the hallway, closer to the main entrance, was blaming us because we told her that we did not know if the building had record of us living there. She said that could be a big problem for us that. She also added that rent is going up every year in general which made me wonder why she said that to us. Therefore, I did not get help from both government offices. Another lawsuit had to do about the board that never paid anything for over twenty years. That also led them to take advantage of us and the others. I called the gentleman at the Public sector on the day I left court after I brought the board on trial on the HP action case. The gentleman at the Public sector may or may not know if the board lived in the buildings. I let the gentleman at the Public sector knew about that. It was the gentleman at the Public sector warned me that the board would come after me as revenge.

Another lawsuit that the board would face was the wrongfulness of the corporation address. What the board reported to the Public sector and in court as information that printed out when I came to court after inspector came to the apartment on the HP action case. The right address of the corporation had been found on November 2013 while I did extra research on my phone about the buildings. There were clues in the first paper that the court gave me on the second HP action case, which I did not make some sense about. I checked the paper again and made personal correction on it myself. I also did correction on what I found out about the CEO/Chairman that passed away. However, the information of the CEO/Chairman that passed away had been updated and changed to some degree which made me wonder who made the changes. These updates and changes occurred in 2014 few months before the holdover proceeding case took effect. Another lawsuit against the board had to do about the bills of the buildings were due. The buildings owed almost three hundred thousand dollars. The board started to build the bills few months after the death of the CEO/Chainman. More bills may seem to come to the buildings such as the light and gas bills. Another lawsuit against the board had to do about the apartments in the buildings, as well as the buildings were not for sale. Another lawsuit was about the apartment that never got any maintenance since my father moved in, as well as damages the private property of the shareholder done by the board. The board ended up being irresponsible, careless, arrogant, and ignorant on that. The CO-OP must reimburse us the money that they owe to us on private maintenance for over thirty years, particularly to reimburse me the money I paid to build the bathroom floor on May 2012.

Another lawsuit that the board faced had to do about the fakeness of the Bylaws and Proprietary Lease, and Stock Certificate. I had no idea if the proprietary lease had it used or applicable in the Co-Ops, particularly about HDFC Co-Ops. The TIL indicated the use of the Bylaws and Apartment lease. I do not know if the apartment lease and proprietary lease were the same or different. The Bylaws, Stock Certificate, and Proprietary Lease happened to contribute on the scam that the board committed on the trial of the holdover proceeding case. I sent copies of the fake Bylaws to Authority, Public sector, and the court knew about it during the trial of the holdover proceeding, but never collected from me on the trial. The board would take responsibility of the proprietary lease that I found on the internet because my father seemed to never have one. The proprietary lease that I found also sent to Authority and the court had it as one of the exhibits I brought in court during the trial of the holdover proceeding case. The board had anything to say to me when they crossed the line. I kept investigating the buildings from October 2013 until May 2014.

Another lawsuit that board would face was about the TIL. The board was not only the ones to get blame for that. The Public sector and Private sector should share the blame on that as well, particularly the Private sector. The gentleman at the Public sector and the Lady at the Private sector never told me about the TIL during the time I was looking for help from them. I found about the TIL when I did some research and download it from the Private sector's website on November 2013. The TIL came out in 1986, two years before the buildings turned into Co-Ops in 1988 and 1989. No one in the buildings seemed to know about the TIL, including my father. The board knew about the TIL and never said anything about it. Another lawsuit had to do about that the board raised the rent illegally.

Another lawsuit had to do about the board called police on me twice, particularly the second time. The police had the intention of forcing me out of the building by claiming that the law of the Co-Op stated that if they do not want me in the apartment, I must leave. It had been said on the Bylaws. How stupid of some police officers could be to get involve into something that was not their business, as well as not a job of the police officers. I spoke with the detective few hours early, concerned about what had happened to my mother a day before. I went to meet with him where exactly where my mother showed what happened to her. I met with the detective on the same spot where my mother told me of what happened to her. I asked the detective about can the police help me with the financial problems of what had been going in the buildings. He responded by saying that it was not a police job because it was not a crime. It seemed wrong and weird that the police involve in the buildings business that day on January 3, 2014. Otherwise the board is looking to make a citizen arrest on us and trying to get help from the police for that. Therefore, calling police on us three times considered more of offenses. Calling police on us considered as harassment, prejudice, and discrimination which led to injustice toward us, particularly on the day of the illegal eviction that took place.

All of the information that I found about the buildings were very useful. I was unable to use them during the trial of the HP action case because they would be irrelevant to the HP action case. The HP action case had to do about who is responsible to fix the apartment. Another lawsuit against the board had to do about all of the three envelopes that the board and their lawyer(s) sent to me illegally. Therefore, I waited until the board brought me in court to use these findings against them on the trial of the holdover proceeding case. The TIL also contradicted a lot of what had been included in these envelops during the HP action case. All my findings had been sent to Authority. These findings also use as evidence and exhibits on the trial of the holdover proceeding. Some of these findings sent to the gentleman at the Public sector. Everything would be explained later on why I sent these findings to the gentleman at the Public sector. The Lady at the Private sector received these envelops by emails during the time I was in court with the board on the HP action cases. The law firm G***** and L*** PLLC knew about the response I sent to them. No wonder why the lawyer came to court to lie in front of the Judge and behaving strange in court because the response I sent to the law firm turned out to be spooky and scary. Therefore, the law firm effectively taken responsibility of their clients since the law firm helped their clients committed perjury, identity theft, falsifies information and documents, as well as knowing all of the problems that occurred in the buildings. There would be more in details about that after part 3.

Response to the two envelops of the cases that the board's lawyers sent to me on the HP action cases sent to these places:

- G***** and l*** PLLC on September 7, 2013 & 10/2013
- Authority on January 2014
- Gentleman at the Public sector on November 2014
- Lady at the Private sector received the bathroom floor situation I wrote sent to her on August 13, 2013 and all the response I send to the Board's Lawyer on the HP action cases on October 2013. The outcome of the inspection only by email, since she was the one who asked to send the outcome of the inspection to her by email. She also received the paper that print out on the day I came to court after inspector came to the apartment, by email. She also received all the HP action court papers that had by sent to me by the board's lawyer(s) by email.
- The Civil Court in downtown Brooklyn had them and must have copies of them after the trial of the holdover proceeding. I sent the rest on October 2014 after I was evicted illegally to add them to the court file. The rest of what I sent happened to be what had been going on the HP action cases, along with the response I sent to the HP action cases.

Response to your letters (referred to the cases)

I send you my response on the court case that you represent your clients on 8/9/13 and 8/29/13 (**names omitted**). Before I have to write what I have to write, I want you to know that I receive the same letters that you send on the case 8/9/13 and 8/29/13. These letters send me on Miss Head's apartment number few days I came from to court twice. The first letter was given to me through Head's son. The second letter was delivered to me by placing it under my door. I began to be a little suspicion about if your clients pretending not living in the buildings, since I hear from outside source that some people never pay for nothing in both buildings for twenty years. The outside source also told me that these people happen to take advantage of my parents. I also want you to know that the first HP action I done and sent to one of your clients (Head) bounced. I received a card from the post office to come it pick it up the first week of September, 2013. I went to pick the letter and found out it was from the head. Another thing that you need to know I live in 2D not 2B. Sending letters like this to the wrong apartment number sound like a set up to me, not a mistake.

I read the same of the second letter that deliver under my door few days after I came from to court. I found few things add on it which they did not add on the first letter. They add on the second of the same letter now. This part is part 8. It has the "Bylaws" part included on it. I am against most of the parts that you included on both papers, particularly part 8, 11, 14, and 22.

Part 8 of the second affirmative defense: Bylaws (the Flows, loopholes, confusion, and invisibility of it)

I want you to know few things about the bylaws. Your clients need to explain themselves why I do not receive the part that says my responsibilities in the apartment. When the problem occurred on the bathroom floor on July 2, 2013 by the super, the super tried to charge me for internal problems. He said to me that he is going to charge me to fix the lit bin (pipe that goes under the toilet), as well as paying for lit bin, after he charged me $ 75 dollars to fix a problem that we did not cause before he damaged the bathroom floor. I told him I must see the Bylaws before I pay for that. He came back to me almost ten minutes later and said that I do not have to pay for that. I have that in more details on the letter that I should have sent to the Civil Court. I asked your client, the president, who live in the other building in apt 3B, a copy of the Bylaws, after the super damaged the bathroom floor I built end of May, 2013, along with other papers. I received the Bylaws from the manager through her daughter. I read the nonsense it has in it which printing many times. I went again to the president's apartment on the last weekend of July 2013, to ask him the rest of the papers that I requested. The president mentioned about the Bylaws and asked me if I see the part that said what my responsibility is. I told him I read everything but I might miss the part that said what my responsibility is. I told the president, I would go back to my apartment to get the Bylaws and show me what my responsibility is. I went and got the Bylaws, and I asked him to show me what my responsibility is. The president kept flipping pages and said to me I do not get the Bylaws, and this is not it. He kind of changes the subject by talking about something else. I asked him to give me the actual copy of the Bylaws, and I still have the copy of by law that the manager gave me. I never receive any new copy of the Bylaws from either the president or manager. One thing I fail to let you know is that the head did not say anything when she found out the problem that occurred in the bathroom floor on July 2, 2013, which happen to be internal problem (lit bin problem). She also sent the super to charge me wrongful fees for that.

Since the Bylaws are included on the second paper that you send me, it does not provide me with basic details, clarity, and specification about what my responsibility is. I want you to know that this apartment paid 32 years of maintenance which exceeding more than $ 130,000 dollars. I wonder where all of this money going, as well as what kind of maintenance that we paid for when we spend money from our pockets to do our own maintenance. Since the paper that you send to me, says the shareholder is responsible for the internal of the apartment without providing enough details, clarity, and specification on that as well. Does that include internal physical structure everywhere in the apartment since the apartment suffers from internal physical structure problem that should have been fixed during the time when the government came to fix some of the apartments in the building, as well as before my father moved in the apartment? My father has been leaving in the apartment few years before the government came to fix some of the apartments in the buildings. His apartment did not get the share of the fixing. He inherited all of the problems since he moved in the apartment in 1981 or 1982. The bathroom floor happens to be one of them. It suffers from internal physical structure problems. The board members (your clients), know about all of the problems. I have more details about that on the letter that I should have sent to the civil court. The board did not do good work in the living room walls and ceiling after the fire that occurred on the apartment above in February 2005 or 2006. These problems are still remained. Since the board claimed that the ceiling is under their responsibility, but they do not do anything about that.

Speaking of the board members (your clients) responsibility, as well as what the Bylaws said on the paper that you send to me is not enough. What your clients said to me is different from one another when it comes to the Bylaws. This is what they say about the bylaws individually to me verbally, as well as the board responsibility. See below.

Manager: says that the internal or inside of the apartment (wall and floor) is the board member responsibility. The ceiling of the apartment is board member responsibility as well. She told me about that after she came in the apartment the second time after the super damage the bathroom floor.

President: says that everything is the shareholder responsibility. He wants to make the ceiling become the shareholder responsibility.

Head: out of everything, but only care about coming with bogus charges on damages to those whom she wants to make money out of. I have that in more details on the letter I should have send to the civil court.

The other part that they need to bring to court is the ancillary document. They also need to send me a copy of it as well. I need to read and analyze it before I go back to court on October 17, 2013. Failure of not providing me with a copy of ancillary document can be a problem for your clients. All they do is making things up because they do not want to take responsibility of anything.

Part 11 of the third affirmative defense (individuals named as Co-respondents are not the Landlord or Owner)

When I came to court on July 31, 2013 after I gave the super a week to comply with the letter I sent to him after he damaged the bathroom floor I build for my parents at the end of May, 2012. Before I sent the letter to him on July 17, 2013, I confronted him about the problem after I spoke with your clients about the problems that they already knew about. I spoke with the president when I came to knock on his apartment door next door on July 16, 2013, since he was away for few weeks. He told me that the super said to him that he found the bathroom floor damaged before he did the work. He also said that I can file lawsuits against the super for the wrongful fees, as well as the damage he caused on the bathroom floor if the super denied the damage. I have the confrontation recorded somewhere, as well as include it on the letter I should have sent to the civil court. The super said that it is the board responsibility to fix the problem. When I came to court to get an advice from a lawyer, and he said that it is the landlord responsibility to fix damages done by the super. When the lawyer asked me about if the building I live in, is a Co-Op. I said yes. The lawyer said it is the board members and the Co-ops responsibility to fix any damages done by the super.

Part 14 of the fourth affirmative defense

I find this is in contradictory with part 8 for two reasons. The first reason is that your clients know all of the problems that happen in this apartment, as well as other apartments and the buildings. All they do is ignore the problems. They raise the rents four to five times already in the name of maintenance, when there is no good maintenance going on in the apartment. They just patch things up and later fall apart. That was what the manager said to me when I told her that the damage that the super left can cause leak on the apartment below. Her response was, she would just patch it up. The second reason is that your clients must explain to the judge why they deliver papers under the doors of the shareholders and tenants in April, 2013 about to contact them if someone claims to be an inspector. I have the paper with me. I find part 14 is in contradictory to part 8.

Part 22 of the sixth affirmative defense

I find this part is all lies since I let the Judge knows it is the super who done the work on the bathroom floor. Your clients know well about that and it can turn against them. I find potential for lawsuit against your clients there. I find part 22 as a false accusation done by your clients in order to make me taking responsibility of the super's mess, as well as taking the fall for the super's mess. Your client should be happy about that I got rid of the biggest evidence for them. Now it is going to be their responsibly since they damage the bathroom floor.

Note: I sent you the copy of the letter that I should sent to the Civil Court. It is attached behind the respond of the court case. Read everything through before you make decision to represent Miss Head in court.

Proposal

Since you and your clients are playing child games because they do not want to take responsibility of anything. Since the apartment never get its fair share of work and maintenance, the board members has to do 70% of the work themselves, I would do 30%. Since the government did not fix my father's apartment, which I did know any reasons why. The board members and the Co-op did not do any repairs and works before my father move in the apartment in 1981 or 1982. I ask your clients for reparation. The lawyer that I spoke with about the issue told me that my responsibility is to buy materials to put on the floor and wall. These materials are woods, ceramic floors and walls. However, since your clients already have done work that definitely put us and the apartment at risk of fire and health issues, they are going to do these works all over again. Since your clients never finish work that they started, these work need to be done as well. See below.

The **kitchen ceiling** and the **bedroom 2 ceiling (Part of the kitchen).** I talk to the inspector who came to inspect the apartment. I send you the record of what the inspector says, as well as what I report. See below. I sent the same information to the person at UHAB. My responsibility is to buy woods for the kitchen floor and bedroom 2 floor. Few parts of the kitchen wall suffer from damages that have been there since my father moved in the apartment. I would buy ceramic tiles to protect the physical structure of the wall in the kitchen.

The living room: the wall and the ceiling are definitely the board members (your clients) responsibility. See below as well.

The outcome of the inspection conducted on 8/21/13

I have to let you know that the inspector could not do anything about the problem of the ceilings that Mr. President built under the ruin of the actual ceilings in one bedroom and the kitchen, probably a week before Thanksgiving in 2010. The inspector told me the board is being smart about that. The board has hidden the problems so that anyone could not see them. The inspector told me that could be a problem for me, and I should have stopped them during the time the work was conducted on the ceilings. I have to let you know that mice have been running in the living room, bedroom, and kitchen ceilings, as well as inside the holes on the living room, bedroom, and kitchen floor, particularly under the heaters and the throughout the kitchen. The inspector told me she can only report by what is visible. Do not worry about the gate at the fires cape because that is our responsibility. I do not put down on the paper to check gates at the windows. I only put down checking windows because the kitchen window is somehow having minor damage for probably seven years. We have to use woods to keep it open from below. One more thing make sure that the president does not make us pay for the fines that the building is about to get for violation. I let you that already he charges us the fees for the lawyers that he took on August 9, 2013. As I said before, what the president is doing is illegal and corrupt.

The living room is still in the mess because they did not do good work on after the fire that occurred above us in 2005 or 2006. The whole ceilings of the apartment are not protected from leaking, as well as the floors of the apartment are not protected from leaking. I have to put tiles on tiles on the apartment's floors to make sure that water does not go down the apartment below us. I do not put light bulb on the living room ceiling for two reasons. The first reason is that I do know if mice chew on the wire and cause fire. The second reason is that the tenants above us making loud noises. These noises are dropping heavy stuffs on the floor in the living room, throwing chairs when they have arguments sometimes, and having intercourse. I confronted them twice about the noise problems. They keep doing it. I reported to the head about that. It seems to me that she never done anything about that. I stopped putting lights in the living room early this year (2013), after I lost three light bulbs in two months. A cheap light bulb can only last two to three months. These light I buy are special lights. One of them can last about four to five years. They are special lights that are design to reduce on the electrical use. The super came and damage one of the light bulbs I put in the bathroom, when he came to fix the lit bin (pipe that goes under the toilet) on the ceiling of the bathroom above us early this year (2013) and end of last year (2012). The whole apartment ceiling suffers from the fire that occurred in 2005 or 2006. The ceiling in the living room suffers the more damage because the fire spread heavily there. I went in the apartment few days after the fire with the super that was there and quit the buildings. The apartment happened to be a scary place in the dark. The whole apartment set on fire.

Bedroom 1: ceiling damage and left neglected by the board members. The problem that occurred during the fire is now appearing on the ceilings few years later after the fire occurred. I started to paint bedroom 1 and stop for now due few problems that are being there. These few problems need to be corrected so that I can finish painting bedroom 1. I already did work on the wall in bedroom 1 since the wall wears out all by itself this May, 2013. The board members (your clients) knew about that. They leave it neglected. I would buy wood to put on the floor in bedroom 1. That is why your clients must explain to the judge in what way the wall of the apartment is under the responsibility of the shareholder, since it stated in the Bylaws.

Hallway: The hallway wall is ok despite the fact that few aspects of it wear out and I corrected that in May 2013. I painted the wall of the hallway in June 2013. I would buy woods to put on the floor.

Bathroom: The bathroom floor is under your clients' responsibility. The wall that locates by the bathtub is uneven, as well as suffers for internal physical structure problem. The bathroom floor suffers from internal physical structure problem. Check for more details on the letter that I should have sent to the Civil Court.

Noting: HDFC puts limits on income on it clients. You cannot go beyond what they require you to make a year. Let your clients know that I would keep record of everything and send them to HDFC since they do not want to give me the address of which HDFC is responsible for the buildings.

"I did send something to one of the HDFC address that I found on the HDFC website, to find out if they were affiliated to 283 and 289 Parkside ave HDFC, along with what few documents of what had been happened on the first HP action case to HPD SCRIE the same day. Therefore, both places sent me all of the documents I sent to them back along with letters. The HDFC place told me that they do not recognize the buildings. HPD SCRIE told me that to call 311 about the problem that happened to the apartment and us. I discovered that each and every HDFC building operating independently. One of the articles I read stated that any buildings can become HDFC, and must follow HDFC rules and regulations. The envelopes that I sent to them happened to send to them probably on October 2013."

Noting: I send you the bathroom floor situation if you want to represent the head in court. There are some questions she needs to answer. See below.

The bathroom floor situation: Letter that should have been sent to the Civil Court.

Date start 7/20/13

Date end 8/13/13

Dear lawyer or Judge

I send you this letter to tell you that I need your help to settle a case about the damage done by the super who live in my building on July 2, 2013, on my bathroom floor. I have been accused of leaks went down on the shareholder's apartment below me due to bad work I heard I done on my bathroom floor at the end of May, 2012. The super and one of the board members, the head (apt 2-B) made such accusation. I told the board member and the super that the leaking was an internal problem. I said that to the super one more time before he removed the toilet. The super blamed the problem on the grease under the toilet and the little loose from the toilet. He asked about what happened to the two screws that hold the ring of the lit bin under the toilet. I told him that the toilet never had any. I even explained to him that the toilet and the floor were in bad condition and there was only one screw hold the toilet before I removed the damage floor and build a new floor last year (end of May 2012). I told the super I bought the second screw for the toilette during the time I built the new floor. I have to let you know that the floor of the bathroom has been damaged before I moved in the apartment in November 15, 1996. My father only knows how long the floor has been damaged when he moved in the apartment in 1981 or 1982. However, my father let my mother and me in charge of the apartment due to his absence in June 2008. All of the board members, the President, and the super know about the damage of the bathroom floor before I rebuild it. Even the person who was in charge of the building (CEO/Chair) knew about the problem before she died from cancer in 2008 (based on what I heard). Even the head's son knew about the floor has been damaged on July 7, 2013 in the morning, to show him about the damage that the super done. He said that he would talk to his mother about that. I never get any respond from him about that. The board members came in the bathroom when there were leaks happened above us many times in the past. None of them never said and did anything about the damage floor, but let that be our responsibility. I also find it unfair and unacceptable because the board raised the rent on us four to five times during the last past six years, when we pay out of our pockets to fix damages in the apartment. We have been told that the floor and the wall of the apartment are our responsibilities. We have to fix them even though if they wear out by themselves. This is not a contract that we sign for. It is more of a verbal contract and a "Bylaws" written by I do not know who. The president, at the other building apt 3B, says the super can charge us to fix anything in our apartment. There are things that we should have never pay for such as add cement or glue under the toilet. At the same time the super and the head said I have to pay for the damage done by the toilet and paid to fix the damage. The super and the shareholder, as well as someone who helped the super that day, were there when the super tried to charge me for lit bin and paid him to put lit bin and fix the floor. He charged me two hundred fifty dollars to do the work and told me the lit bin cost around one hundred fifty dollars. He also said that he charged other few shareholders in the building, as well as in the next building for the same problem. He also said that it is said in the Bylaws. I told him I would give the money, but I need to read the Bylaws first. Around ten minutes later, he came and knocked on my door and said that I did not have to pay for the lit bin; it is the board's responsibility to pay for that.

That is what happened on July 2, 2013. The super (name omitted), charged us seventy dollars for leaks that did not cause by us. The leaking problem caused by the lit bin (pipe under the toilet). He also damaged the floor I paid to build last year (May 2012) when he drilled on the floor. I send you the copy of the letter I sent to the super, along with dates on it. The letter has to do about filling lawsuit against the super. The super thought I was kidding when I told him I would file a lawsuit against him if he does not give the seventy dollars back for the wrongful fees and not fixing the damage he left on the bathroom floor. The president and the board members did not want to do anything about the problem. The president told me that I can file a lawsuit against the super when I talked to him about the problem on July 16, 2013. The super even lied to them about everything. He said to them that he found the floor like that. When I confronted him on July 17, 2013 at 9am, about the damage that he left on floor, could cause leaks now. He said the damage on the floor is not his responsibility; the board members are responsible for that. I have the confrontation recorded somewhere as proof. There are more details on the letter I send to him on Wednesday July 17, 2013 about when the plumber came back on Sunday July 7, 2013 to check the lit bin late on the afternoon around 6pm. Another board member, the manager (apt 1-C), said she and the other board members would have a meeting with me and the super to see how the matter could have been solved. That meeting never took place. That meeting should have been taken place on July 11, 2013, after she came in the bathroom to show her the damage done by the super on July 10, 2013, on the afternoon. That meeting should have taken place at 7 pm on July 11, 2013. Therefore, none of them want to take responsibility of the damage done by the super. Even the super does not want to take responsibility of his damage. I do not really want to sue anyone;

I just want the damage done by the super to get fix. They would have to pay the person who done the work for me, as well as pay for materials to fix the damage. If that is not working, I would sue the super or the board in order to make the money to fix the damage. I also do not know how deep the super drilled and damaged the bathroom floor. The only way to tell is by removing the toilet. If nothing done about the damage now, it can become major problem in the future. However, everything changes when I went to court in the building that locates in downtown Brooklyn on July 31, 2013. I spoke with a lawyer about the problem. He told me the landlord is responsible for any damage that the super caused. Since Miss Head happens to be the head of the board, I have to go to court with her.

I have to go to court on December 19, 2013 because I have cases the head. I have filed a small claim of $ 2000 dollars against her. She has to pay me $ 950 dollars that I spend to build the floor (labor, materials, transportation). She has to pay me $200 dollars for getting rid of the pieces of concrete (labor and transportation). She has to pay me $ 400 dollars for my labor because I carried all the 6 bags of broken pieces of the bathroom floor outside. She has to pay me the $ 70 dollars that the super charged me for the wrongful fees. The rest of the claim is about everything that they put me through, as well as that is not the first time the super damage my property. He sabotaged the pipe under the bathroom sink one Saturday morning afternoon on April 2013, after I have been accused of causing clog. The head send the super to charge me for the clog that I did not cause, as well as charge me for the leak it caused on the apartment below me. The whole debris came from above and somehow clogs on my pipe. I fought back and they left me alone. I send this letter and with the copy of the court date behind the letter. In the mean time I have HP action coming on the way to the board members. That is the second HP action that I am doing because I made a mistake. I find out about that when I went to court on Friday August 9, 2013. The Judge told me that I would lose if I go on trial. I was not clear enough about what I was doing. I am doing this for the first time. I began to see I how to do it right. The judge decided to close the case without prejudice. I also send you the copy of the letter.

Noting: on the day I removed the damage floor in the bathroom, there are internal problems and complications that the person who did the work and I face. I do not know if I am responsible or not for the internal problems that I found. These internal problems have to do about that the bathroom floor suffers from internal structures problems from the inside the floor. The wall of the bathroom also affects from the inside. We have to find ways around them in order to build the new floor with strength and stability. We removed approximately 200 to 300 pounds of concrete. I even paid to get rid of the broken pieces of the bathroom floor few days after the work done. The board members and the president knew I was going to redo the floor of the bathroom before I done it and during the days that I done it. The president gave me few garbage bags to put all the broken pieces of the bathroom floor inside. The garbage bags that he gave me were not strong enough to hold all the broken pieces of the bathroom floor. I have to buy strong bags design only for constructions in order to put the broken pieces of the bathroom floor inside. I have to double each bag to put the broken pieces of the bathroom floor inside. I ended up getting rid of six bags of broken pieces of the bathroom floor. I have to remind you again that the board members say that the floor and the wall of the apartment are the shareholder responsibility. They must pay to get them fix. The board and the super say that the shareholder can choose anyone to do the job for him or her. It has been written in the Bylaws. The person who built the floor did not want to build it for me due to the fact he is an outsider. I asked the super of the building I would pay him to build the floor for me. He said yes, until he changed his mind by saying he did not have time for that. The super said to me that he was worried more about his son's soccer player practice. However, the person who built the floor for me said that the super said to him that the super did not want to do the job because he was afraid to get stuck with it. The person who builds the floor and makes it better than it was before. The super came on July 2, 2013 and damage the floor.

I find out that there are unequal treatments going in this building because some shareholders getting better treatment than other shareholders. Those unequal treatments have been going on since the day my father moved in the apartment in 1981-1982. My father paid and we paid more than $120,000 dollars in rent and maintenance and yet we still spend money in our pockets to fix damages. My father used to tell stories about the apartment never used to have windows and heaters when he moved in. He has to get help from family and friends to put windows and heaters in the apartment. I find it so strange that the board members in the building raise the rent on us four to five times within the past five years for maintenance. The board members raise the rent and say that the board of directors of the buildings raises the rent when we do not know the name of the board of directors of the buildings. We never received any letter directly from the board of directors. I was a little suspicious about the rent hikes in 2009 when I call someone from the Private sector to find out the reason why the rent went up that year. The person said to me that the shareholders made the decision to raise the rent. I was surprised because we never make that decision to raise the rent. I kept some of the paper about the rent hikes this year (2013). If the board members said that the shareholders make choice or vote in meeting to raise the rent, I would say no because there were no meeting going for that. After what happened to me July second 2013, I began to see that the board in my building has been control by bunch people who have been arrogant, ignorant, negligent, carelessness, and irresponsible. No wonder why they do not want inspector to come in the buildings. I have a letter that they sent to each and every shareholder on April 2013 about not letting any inspectors come in their apartments. I find it unfair and unacceptable because we pay our rent on time and never owe on rent, and yet we still receive poor treatments. I conclude the letter now and I am hoping to hear from you soon. I am taking care of what my father was unable to take care. I have a letter that I wrote for him and made him signed it before he left the apartment in August 18, 2008. He let me and my mother in charge of the apartment during his absence.

Sincerely

My name omitted

Note: My address, super's, and the board addresses are omitted for the purpose of the book.

Part 4

Repetition

I found it very strange of the first lawyer that the board had, using the same strategy about that I was not the shareholder in front of the Judge on the small claim case, behind a close door. The lawyer knew that I am the son of the shareholder already. The lawyer tried to play the unpredictable and unexpected move on me again. The lawyer trapped with the repetition when I opened my mouth and told him that this had no relation on the case. What the lawyer was trying to do before we faced the Judge was asking for the "application". The lawyer asked for application in order to have the case dismissed, discontinued, or closed. I made a shocking discovery about the board changed the head's last name into something else. I had the receipt and paper work about the way I filed for the small claim. The court should at least send me a letter to tell or notify me about the changes that had been made. The court clerk got the nerve to tell me that it was my responsibility to fix the changes, when I came to court next day after the first round, to find out how these changes had been made. The court should be the one to get blame, as well as being irresponsible for the changes that had been occurred. The clerk also got the nerve to tell me that I should have told the Judge about the changes. I was also under suspicion that the board's lawyer also contributed to the changes as well. That changes had been going on the second envelop that the board's lawyer sent to me on the second HP action case, which I thought was a mistake. I was under suspicion that was the same thing the board and their lawyer(s) did on the HP action cases about changing information about us. The court seemed to allow them to make the changes as well, which made me wonder why.

I found the board and their lawyer(s) got the guts and nerves to use fake names. Once the lawyer found out about that he trapped with everything and the Judge said that the case continued for trial, the lawyer talked to the board outside of the courtroom. That made me wonders what the board and their lawyer talked about. I was under suspicion that the lawyer did not really tell the board about what had been going on in all of the court cases. I also wondered why the lawyer was the only one showed up in front of the Judge, instead of showed up with his client. Was the lawyer made the decision to tell his client not to show up, or was the client made the decision not to show up, but placed all her faith on the lawyer about taking care of everything? However, the lawyer tried to save himself from all of the problems that his clients and he had been produced. The lawyer had enough time to get out of the problems since the HP action cases, when I sent response to all the lies, false allegation, and contradiction that his clients and he sent to me. I warned the lawyer about the bathroom floor issue which I sent to the lawyer along with the response. I sent the bathroom floor issue as cases I had against his clients. I also sent bathroom floor issue to People's Court almost a week and half later, after I received a letter from them concerning about the small claim case I had against Miss Head.

I had no idea how People's Court and the Judge found record about the small claim case I filed against the head. I sent the bathroom floor situation to People's Court since I received the letter from them first. I was under suspicion that the downtown court in Brooklyn must have had the bathroom floor issue as well. There will be more details about that at the end of part four about the outcome of the small claim case. The board's lawyer knew about everything that had been going on. Therefore, he ignored everything by trying to pretend that nothing never actually happened. All of the lawyer(s) care about was to make money on their clients and later their clients want us to pay for that money with a huge amount of interest behind it. All the board had been doing was to use the buildings finance to fund their lawyers and later on made us pay for that, along with a huge interest on top of that. I do not think that we were the only one the board done that to in the buildings. The lawyer's fees also contributed to the debt that the buildings owed invisibly. I wondered how many people out there who are in position of power, using the their buildings' finance to fund their lawyers and made the tenants pay for that, by using the rent hikes as an excuse, advantage, and pretext to make up for their lawyers' fees and maximized profit. The board's lawyer(s) thought they would leave mess by letting their clients to take the fall and walk away free. That I would not effectively let it happened. I made sure that the board's lawyers never escaped the problem that they and their clients created, by blaming their clients for the problem.

I use to hear from few people saying that lawyers blame their clients when they are unable to deal with the problem that they and their clients created. No wonder why I kept record about what had been going on outside of the courtroom and let the board's lawyer(s) knew about them. I let the board's lawyer knew about his clients called Police on me twice (12/31/13 & 1/3/14); after I received anonymous mail from the board that the board and their lawyer (G***** & L*** PLLC) almost a week later in January, 2014, after calling police on us. The anonymous letter was the beginning of trying to get possession of the apartment from us illegally. The board's lawyer(s) were also helping the board doing it. The board's lawyer(s) knew the buildings are a Co-Op. Therefore the board's lawyer(s) decided to help the board used the Co-Op as landlord. The board and their lawyer(s) used another anonymous address (KPS) to send me illegal documents. I sent the same response that I sent to the board's lawyer to KPS as well. It was the same response that I sent to both parties ended up used as response collected in court before the trial of the holdover proceeding. I send another response to the board's lawyer after I received another anonymous letter sent by KPS. I send another letter again to the board's lawyer after I received another anonymous letter from KPS. The last two letters were collected during the trial of the holdover proceeding. I sent the three responses at once to the board's lawyer on May 2014 few weeks after I was actually served by the board and their lawyer(s). I thought the board and their lawyer(s) were bluffing and playing about going through with the "John Doe" and "Jane Doe" against me, as ways to scare me off the trial of the small claim.

The responses that I sent to the board's lawyer(s) about the "John Doe" and "Jane Doe" had been sent along with the copy of the paper that the court gave me and the board during the HP action case along with the copies of August and December 2013 rent receipts. KPS only received the copy of the HP action paper that the court gave me to prove to them that there was no landlord in the buildings. The main reason which led the board to call police on us on January 3, 2014 had to do about the note I wrote on the December 2013 receipt when I made January 2014 payment. The note was delivered under the president's apartment and to the head with the January 2014 payment. The board was angry by the note. These receipts I sent to the board's lawyer(s) also sent to the Public sector, lady at the private sector by email, Authority, and collected in court during the trial of the holdover proceeding as exhibits. I sent the copies of all the 2013 rent receipt, along with two other old copies of payment that the other board members signed payment to Authority, Public sector, and collect on the trial of the holdover proceeding as exhibits. I did so in order to prevent the other board members denial of never sign receipts for us.

One day on March 2014, someone rang our apartment's bell. I went down to the lobby to open the door. I do not know for how long the buildings had been out of buzzing system at the door. When I opened the door, the lady came in all the way where the mail boxes located. She asked me about where the super lived. I showed her where the super lived. I also showed her where the board lived. She knew effectively that some of the apartments in the buildings rented out particularly to Caucasians. She was absolute right about that. I did not know who sent her in the buildings. I did not even ask her where she came from. There was another person witnessed when the lady came in. The witness was a lady who lived in the shareholder's apartment below us. She came in the apartment below us and I did not know if she was a relative of the shareholder. Even Miss Head had someone live in her apartment. I did not know who that person was. The board even tried to use that problem against me on the first envelop that their lawyer sent to me on the HP action case. It was defense 11. I was confused by it. I do not know if the board stated or meaning that I had someone lives in my apartment without their knowledge, which happened to be Miss Heads' apartment. The envelope had my name and sent to apartment 2B. I regretted that I did not sent response to that because I did not know if the problems, issues, and predicaments would get that far. That also proved that Miss Head was under suspicion of taking rent from the person. That also proved the wickedness of the board to set me up with an apartment that I did not live in.

The board and their lawyer changed defense 11 that was in first envelop to something else on the second envelop that they sent to me. I wondered why they did such changes. Defense 11 was not the only defense that they change. Defense 8 happened to be adjusted on the second envelope that the board's lawyer sent to me. It seemed to be that the board wanted to change things because they found out that they trapped with them. All of these changes that the board and their lawyer made on the envelopes effectively prove how sneaky, slicky, and sleazy they were. No wonder why the Judge who gave me the paper to protect myself on the first HP action case created a transition to the second HP action case so that everything that the board and their lawyer sent to me can be used in court. Above all these envelopes sent to me illegally which effectively used against the board and their lawyer(s) because that had been counted as forging documents, and perjury committed by the board and their lawyers.

The reason why the board charged us for the lawyer's fees despite the fact that the Judge putted on paper that the board should pay for their lawyer, may have to do about what had been stated on the proprietary least. The proprietary least that I found online stated that the tenants must pay the lawyer fees of that of the landlord. It seemed to be that whether the landlord is guilty of any wrongdoings toward the tenants, the tenants must pay the landlord for his/her lawyer fees. I even heard from the shareholder who was affected by the fire July 2010 fire said to me one day that some people in the buildings paid the lawyer fees to the board. That sound to me that some people in the buildings were afraid of the board which led to harbor the board. That was the reason why the board established total power, privilege, oppression, discrimination, injustice, and disrespectful on everyone that was not part of their families. No wonder why the inspector who came in the apartment during the second HP action case, said that never went against the board. I have to always put smile on my face when I saw them. The inspector also added that the board would raise the rent on us if the board fixed the apartment. The inspector was right about that. The first envelop sent to my father on 9/13/13 and received on 9/18/13, with paper that looked like Bylaws or Proprietary Lease had one part stated that "the corporation can send its agents to collect money from the shareholder for maintenance, and raise the rent on the shareholder if the corporation repairs the apartment". No wonder I gave the board and their lawyer(s) a proposal. The board would commit wrongdoings towards anyone whether or not the board got respect from some or anyone. That proved how the board did not have respect for the Court, and the board's lawyer also contributed to the problem of not having respect for the Court. They thought they can do whatever they want. However, I will not be surprised if Authority let them get away with all the wrongdoings the board had been created for over twenty years.

The receipt of the Small Claim sent to Authority along with all the 2013 rent receipts and all the envelopes I received before the holdover proceeding case. The downtown court had the same thing that I sent to Authority and served as evidence and exhibits on the trial of the Holdover Proceeding case. The gentleman from HPD received everything as well. The lady at UAHB also received everything as well by email. All parties received the notes I wrote on the December 2013 receipt which led the Board called police on me. The board's lawyer knew about them as well.

"The reason why the board accused my mother of committed voodoo, particularly the president, by throwing water in front of the building, was that all Haitians associated with voodoo. My mother is a person who does not have understanding about what has been going on around her, particularly living in a City that full with different races and cultures. My mother is also a type of woman who likes to do whatever she wants to do and do not want me and anyone to tell her that she is wrong. I cannot stop her from doing what she is doing for two reasons. The first reason has to do about that my mother always has holy water ever since I was born and continued to do so. Therefore, it will be hard for her to let go off of that no matter what I said to her, particularly about keeping what she is doing in the dark, not in the light where people can see and have wrong thinking about what she is doing. The second reason has to do about that my mother is a tedious and stubborn woman and does not care about what people say about what she does with the holy water. Few of our relatives, friends of my mother from church, and people in the buildings knew about the holy water issue. My mother does not know how serious and deadly that the holy water issue can cause to her. My mother does not know that some people can use that as an excuse, advantage, and pretext to come after her, particularly when Haitians happen to be the few of the most nation or people suffered on earth to some degree. I told her about what could have happened many times. The respond she always gives is that God is there to protect her, as well as never let anything happen to her. She claims that she is doing God's work. I even find it absurd that my mother telling me that it is not me going out there taking care of my business, only God taking care of all my business for me. Despite the fact that I talked to my mother about what the President told me in a savage and barbaric matters in front the super, who was there and smiled as if he took pleasure out of that, my mother never listen. She had

the belief that evil is around her, and the holy water is a way to chase the evil away. My mother laughed at what happened and said to me by the president, which was a serious problem that the board wanted to cause for us. She should have stopped that completely, but unable to do so because of the conviction that she has about holy water chase evil away. Therefore, I have to deal with her issue because the board used a different plan to deal with the issue. The board wrote on paper accused my mother of spraying stuff in front of the building that affected the health of the tenants. The board wrote on paper was different than what the president said to me that morning. There was no names and signature of who sent the letter to us."

• Sent to Authority and the Court may have had it after the eviction took place.

Name omitted

Address omitted for the purpose of the book

1/22/14

Letter to ## Precinct

I want you to know that the people who control the buildings (addresses omitted) called police on me twice for no reason because they do not want to deal with problems that they cause in the financially. Their names are (omitted). They called Police on me December 31, 2013 after I went to the president's apartment to talk to him about the illegal fees that he and the others charged us. They called Police on me when the police arrived, his family were not being specific about who came to knock on their door and why. I knew that the president's family called Police for me because I was outside when the Police Officers came in and out of the building at (other building). One of the Police Officers asked to approach him while they were in the police car. They asked me that someone called for police due to the reason that the person knocked on their door. I asked the Police Officer which apartment. Was it apartment 3B? He said yes. I let the Police Officer knew that they call Police for me due to the reason that they charged me for illegal fees. I let the Police Officers knew that the apartment that they came from, that is where the President live with his family. I let the Police Officer knew that this is a CO-OP place. The President and others charged me for maintenance that we never received, as well as damage our property and did not want to fix it. The Police t told me what to do about that, after I told them that I have been in court for the HP action.

On January 3, 2014, the President and the others called Police on me after I made payment for January 2014, and staple the money order along with a copy of the receipt for the payment I made December 2013. I wrote a note on the copy of the December 2013 receipt to find out why we have to pay the illegal fees for. I give the money order and the copy of the receipt to the head's son who live across me (2B), and I went next door to deliver the other copy of receipt under the president's door (next building at 3B). They called police on me again. The two Police Officers that came in the building rang my bell. I went downstairs and found out they involved at what is not Police business. I tried to explain to them what was going on. I let Police Officers knew that the people who damage the bathroom floor do not want to fix it. One of the head, manager and the super, were there trying to see what happened and report to head and president. The Police Officers told me to go to court, when I told them that I have been court and nothing works. All I received from the Police Officers were threat and fear, particularly from the female Police Officer. The Police Officers do not know about the same people who called Police on me, live in the buildings, as well as use their apartments as offices. The Police Officers, particularly the Female Police Officer were loud and said that I would be arrested if I go in the other building for trespassing. The Police Officers did not know that everyone who live in both buildings (address omitted) have access in both buildings because they pay for them, even though some people may not pay their fair share. The shareholders have power than the tenants in the buildings. The female Officer was disrespected and oppressed toward my mother, when my mother came down stairs trying to explain to the Police Officers what bothered her with an expression of sad feeling on her face. My mother and I were not happy after the Super damaged the bathroom floor that I built May 2012. The people who are in charge (the board) did not want to be held responsible for the super's mess. Therefore the female Police Officer said to my mother aggressively, go back upstairs. The Female Police Officer is an African American, and the Male Police Officer is a Caucasian.

I went to the precinct the same day, to report what happened. The Police Officer I talked to said that I could not make report about that because it is not a crime. I let the Police Officer knew that I have been threaten by their fellow Police Officers at my building. Noting that the people who are in charge of the buildings said to the Police Officers that they would not accept payment for the apartment from us.

Noting: anyone called by the last name (omitted) are the people responsible for the buildings (address omitted). They have been screwing things in the buildings finances, and they do not want to deal with the consequences. They make their rules when they are not follow universal rules of the CO-OPS. They tried to have the Police at their sides now.

Sincerely

My name omitted

Names and addresses of the board are omitted

The outcome of the Small Claim:

When I came to court on December 17, 2013, the defendants' lawyer asked for application and I got transfer from one courtroom to another. The defendants were in court all happy, made me wondering why they were happy. The head's last name had been changed into something else, which that was not the way I had it done. It was not a mistake because I had the receipt on how it was done. The other defendants contributed to that changes I knew that for facts. I asked a lawyer in the courtroom about what application was. He explained to me right away. He also said that it is depended on the judge whether to continue with the case or not, as well as what has been said to the judge to continue the case. The defendants' lawyer used the same strategy that he used on the HP action case about that I am not the shareholder of the apartment, after I represented my case to the judge. I said to him that was totally unrelated to the case. I showed the judge the pictures of the bathroom floor and wondering who was going to pay for the damage. I let the Judge knew that could care less about the money, but the defendants did not want to do anything about the damage, as well as the bathroom floor suffered from internal physical structure and water could go down quickly on the shareholder that lives below me. The Judge said that could be a big problem. I continued saying that the money that I want back is to reinvest on the floor for materials in case the defendants did not want to pay money on materials. The defendants' lawyer said that his clients are not in charge. I said to the judge yes his clients were in charge. I said where did his clients' offices are located. The judge said that said the case proceeded on April 10, 2014. I also denied the defendants' lawyer when he said that his clients had cases me. I let the judge knew that he lied in front of the judge when he said that he did not receive the response I sent to him about the false allegations and lies that his clients had against me on the HP action case. When I received the receipt for December 2013 payment I made for my father on December 31, along with illegal maintenance fees that the President putted on the receipt. I decided to go to his apartment in the other building to talk to him about the illegal maintenance fees. His father was inside talked to me without opened the door inside his apartment. He said that he did not know where he was.

Nearly half hour later police showed up. I knew for fact that they called police on me. I was outside waiting for the police to come out. The Police Officer who was driving the police car, called me to approach him. When I did so, they asked me if I knew anything about the reason why police had been called in the other building. I asked them was it apartment 3B called police. The Police Officer said yes. I let him knew that they called police for me, and the apartment that called the police was where the President lived. I let them knew that this is a CO-OP. I let the police officers that they called police on me because of the illegal maintenance fees that the president charged us and did not want to deal with the problem they caused. I even showed them the receipt. He took the quick glimpse at the receipt. I told him that I had filed HP action against the buildings and those who run the buildings. The police told me exactly what the lawyer at that HP action would never do anything about the problem. He told me called the department of buildings. I even let the Police Officer knew that I called 311. He said that 311 would never do anything. When I called Department of Building on January 2, 2014, I had been told over the phone that the Department of Building does not take care of CO-OP business and directed me to 311. The lawyer I paid visit told me that the HP action would not do anything. The lawyer even told me story about CO-OP cases that she had held for so many years and told me that she said to her clients that was how CO-OPs operated when her clients complained about the problem that they faced in their buildings. She even told me about what I found out on my research about some shareholders are taking advantages on other shareholders such as raising rents on some shareholders, as well as others are fixing their apartments while other apartments remained unfix. I let her knew that that is what happen in the buildings I live, particularly about the head, which has the most expensive wood floors in her apartment. Her wood floors changes color when the lights are on. The lawyer told me that I went to the wrong court for them. I should have to go to the Spring Court for them (or Supreme Court). When she looked at the court paper that sent to me by the defendants' lawyer, she said that I have cases against the Government.

When I made the January 2014 payment for the apartment, I wrote a note of warning on the copy of the December 2013 receipt. What I sent before along with part A of the report I sent was the second version of it. I sent the first version of the copy of the receipt, along with part B of the report. I made two copies. I stapled one copy along with the money order payment I made for January 2014. I gave it to the head's son since he opened the door, not her to collect the money order from me (apt 2-B). I went next door and delivered the other copy under the door of the president's apartment (apt 3-B). The head's son came and knocked on my door and tried to give the money order back along with a piece of paper. They told me that thank you and they do not want to me live in the apartment anymore. I told them what kind of right do they have by saying "piece of sh**" after? The super was there when I said that. The head, manager, and president called police on me. When the police arrived and rang my bell. The head and the president did not come at the lobby. The manager and the super were there waiting to see what the outcome would be so that they could figure out their next move. The Police officer, a female African American, said that the proprietary least says that if the board did not want me in the building I must leave. She added that the CO-OP operates by only sending letters. She also added that the money that has been collected for rents, are only to do fixing of the buildings (**which they never really fix**). I let the Police Officer knew that the super had been damaged the bathroom floor and the people in charge did not want to do anything about that. The Police Officer said to go to court. I said to the Police Officer that I done all of what she said to me already, but they did not work. However the Police Officers and the manager and the super did not know in what way I said "they did not work" in the context that meant by "they did work" were. Here my elaboration on them. They did not want to compare their Proprietary Least with mine when I asked them to do so during the trial on 12/3/14. I also went by what the lawyer I paid her visit at her office on 12/6/14, as well as what the Police Officer said to me on December 31, 2013. When I had the both HP-actions done, the president happened to be the one to show up in court, without the others (head and manager) to come along. He showed up to court with the others on October 17, 2013, after the outcome of the inspection, as wells as after the HP-action paper printed out which I sent copy of along with other papers stapled together, on the first set of report I sent already. The manager showed up in court on October 17, 2013 and did not stayed when she saw me in the courtroom. She did not even show up at all during the trial (**I sent copy of the trial paper**). I did not think that the president showed the manager and the head about the HP action paper that has information about the Buildings, which the court found from HPD website. The lawyer (**G***** and L*** PLLC and LLP**) knew about the paper as well. The paper stated that the Corporation located in the building I lived instead in his apartment in the other building. I sent the copy of it to the lady at UHAB electronically. The president is the brain all along on everything. He is trying to save his own skin. The police officers where rude and prejudice, particularly the African American police officer, who threaten to arrest me if I went next door (next building). The female Police Officer was also rude and prejudice toward my mother when my mother came downstairs by showing feeling and emotion, almost look crying in front of the police officers, to which the police officer confused them as a sign of threat. My mother does not speak English well, but does the best she could to tell the police officers the same thing I said to them about the damage done by the super on the bathroom's floors and come to see it, which they refused to do so, by pointing fingers on the super. The female police officer said to my mother with anger to go upstairs. The female police officer accused everyone of being loud which she failed to pay attention that the building is too echoes when anyone speak. The female police officer ended up speaking loudly, and even said that she would talk loudly before she did so. The female police officer threaten of arrested me for trespassing if I go in the next building. We pay maintenance for both buildings as well as keys to open both front of the buildings. Even people who may not pay their fair share have same privileged just like us and everyone who paid. It is now become illegal for me to go next door (next building) to talk some of the shareholders despite we pay for both buildings.

When I called the Precinct (## Precinct), I made a strange discovery. I talked to the operator at the precinct and found out that the phone number that was giving to me as contact number for the head before I went to court for the first time, happened to be belong by someone named Thompson. Maybe the others might change their phone numbers as well. When I went to the precinct trying to file complain on the police officers who threaten me that I would get arrested for trespassing, they told me no and I could not filed for complain because it is not a crime. One Friday morning of the same week, I was on my way out, the president and the super were standing outside of the other building. It was raining that Friday and went back inside to get my umbrella. By the time I got back inside, the president called out hey aggressively, and made me wondering why. He kept coming and got inside the building I lived in, accusing my mother came out with a bucket of water and threw it in front of the building, that caused it turned into ice and slippery. I knew that is a lie because my mother is not like that and my mother has fractures on some of her fingers. The president told me that the super saw that on camera and reported to him. I told him that was a lied. He also accused my mother of performing voodoo in front of the building, to which I knew what he was trying to refer to, as well as talking about something to which he did not know anything about. I told him that my mother is a Christian and has holy water in a very small bottle of shampoo to spray few squirt when she comes out sometime in the morning to go to church. My mother even laughs about that when I told her about it. My mother sometime felt evil presence from one of the trees that is located by the side walk. She squirts holy water out to chase the evil spirit away. She told me she done that when she feels the evil spirit comes around. She also said she never squirt holy water during raining day. The super probably saw my mother done that in front of him and used that as an advantage to commit lies. I even let my mother knew not to do anything like that in front of the building because people might get wrong idea about her doing before I was confronted by the president. She never listens. My mother even squirts holy water inside the apartment three to four times a month. Who to blame here, my mother or Christianity? She is my mother and some of her abilities pass to me through birth (genetic). However I sent a copy of the letter sent by the board with another false accusation. What the Board put on papers totally different from what the president said that morning. I have been warned by others that the board and the super like to make things up and lies, particularly the president. When I got out of the apartment the same morning, the president kept saying the same thing about my mother committed act of voodoo out loud in front of the building and called me stupid. The super was there when he said that, with a smile on his face. I told him he is far more stupid than I do, and come to fix the apartment because we pay maintenance every month for that.

On January 16, 2014, I received a letter which I sent a copy of on the first set of the report I sent already. The one that said **"John Doe and Jane Doe"** in front of the envelope. I sent it along without the response I sent to G***** and L*** PLLC (preparer) and to KPS (sender). I sent response to both of the places certified mails. I sent my response in both places when I had to pick up a certified letter sent by the board with a message that said my father must be the only one who can come to pick it up on January 18, 2014, no one else. The board claimed that they work for the Government and it is a Government case. My father must show identification to pick up the letter. How could they do such thing when the board knew that my father has been absent for so many years, and let my mother and I in charge of the apartment. I had to go to some problems to get that letter. When I opened the letter and I saw that they returned the January 2014 payment I made for the apartment for my father, along with two letters. One of the letters had to do about another false accusation about my mother. I sent you the copies of the letters along with the copy of the money order. I even sent the bathroom floor situation and response to the HP action I sent to G***** and L***, to KPS. I sent my response to G***** and L*** and to KPS the same day I was at the post office to pick up the letter sent to my father, January 18, 2014. I even went to the place (KPS) on next day, after I received the letter. All they told me they are the processor and did not want to see any proof from me. The same letter sent to me, but to pick it up at the post office without the **"John Doe and Jane Doe"** written in front of the envelop and sent it without my father's name misspelling on it on January 31, 2014. I did not send my response on the second time because it is the same thing sent to me before.

When I got to court on April 10, 2014, the defendants' lawyer and the head, and I went in small room inside the courtroom, with an attorney who represented the judge due to the reason of scarcity of Judges to handle all small claim matters or cases. I use the HP action cases again to have connection with the small claim. I let the attorney knew about the other problems the apartment has, especially about the bathroom floor. The attorney told me to stop there, to have the defendants' lawyer turns to talk. He said that his clients have cases against me because I am not the shareholder. He said that the proprietary least said that his clients have to renew the list of everyone who lives in the buildings and I should get kick out. He said that the proprietary least said it. He said that his law firm represents his clients all the way to the end of the HP action. The lawyer made it sounds like he never being in court representing his clients, but sent somebody else to represent his clients. He came with the **"John Doe and Jane Doe"** paper in court without the envelope. I cut him off on everything he said, by saying that they were not true. I said to him that the proprietary least never said anything about the son of the shareholder should get kick out. I said the Bylaws is fake because the same thing printing many times over, despite they said that the Bylaws is 40 pages instead of more than 40 pages. I said to him that the wife of the shareholder is there and the shareholder let his wife and son in charge of the apartment. They said that my father never use the apartment as his primary address. I showed the attorney the papers that had information about the buildings, particularly the one that print out during the HP action case, the defendants' lawyer asked to see. I showed it to him and said that he knew about it. He got so mad, said that he did not like what I did and threatened to make me pay the lawyer's fees in front of the attorney who represented the Judge. I let the attorney knew that the people who are in charge are the board of directors, board members, and shareholders after she asked me to see how and where the payment went to. I showed the attorney the paper that the first Judge gave on the first HP-action. The attorney read it out loud in front of the defendants' lawyer and Miss Head's. The court officer opened the door and said that the judge said that was enough. The court officer happened to be the same court officer that was in the courtroom during the trial of the HP-action case on 12/3/14. I let the defendant's lawyer and the head knew that I sent all the papers I received from their lawyers and some recordings to the Justice Department. I told the defendants' lawyer in front of the attorney (the one represented the Judge) that I could care less about the money.

I sent response to G***** & L*** before I went to court, the defendants' lawyer sat in the small room pretending that he never received anything from me. I sent responses certified mails. **I sent copies of the certified mails I sent** when I was in court for the HP-action and small claim. The manager and the president were in court as well.

Buildings name omitted for the purpose of the book

Where the finances of the buildings might be going

After I did research and find out about the board could use the finances of the buildings for their private gain. The lawyer who has her office around the neighborhood I live telling me that is what happened in CO-OPS because some people in CO-OPS use the finances of the buildings for their benefits. I would explain briefly about everyone who in charge individually. Noting that what I have on this paper may sound as an invasion of privacy, which is not.

The President: The president does not have a job. He has more than 5 relatives living in his apartment. As I mentioned before about saying to that he putted his wife name on the apartment he lives in due to the restriction of income. I find that ironic because he and the others (Head, Manager, and the lady at the Private sector) said that a person must make as minimum $35000 a year to stay in one bedroom apartment, in the meeting that took place nearly a week in a half before thanksgiving 2013. That sounds like invasion of privacy. They even set their rules for nonfamily if the spouse; child of the shareholders and/ or the relative of the shareholder want to live in the shareholder's apartment when the shareholder passed away. Or they may choose to kick anyone of them out if they choose to do that illegally. I would explain later on what I found what one of their relatives (not the president's relatives) said to me about what happened with the child of the shareholder who used to live next to me (apt: 2C). As someone with maybe no basic income could afford to have two cars, as well as one of his children/ child (son) (I do not know how many children he has). The license plate number of his car is (Plate number omitted). He also denied that he did not leave in the other building during the time I was in court for the HP action, year 2013. He confessed in court 6/16/14 that he lived in the other building (3B) in court 6/16/14. I also do not know if his son has a decent job to drive the car that he is driving as well. He even fixed his apartment makes me wondering where he gets the money to do that. He also intends to keep his car. That was what he said to me, early January 2013, after he and the others raised the rent.

Head: Her son does not do anything with his life. He may not have a decent job. He has about two children with his girlfriend. Who knows how many children he might have out there without knowing about that? How is he able to pay for the Apple smart phone he has if he does not have a job? How the head has money to fix her apartment floors. As I mentioned before, she has the most expansive hard wood floors in her apartment. Her wood floors change color at night, particularly when there is a bright light shine on her floors. The head has relative living in the next building if I am not mistaking. The work that she has done in her apartment occurred in nearly 3 years after the CEO/Chair, passed away. She has to prove where she got the money from to do the renovation that she made in her apartment. Her son even said to me one day that he did not live in the building during the time I was in court with them for the HP action cases, year 2013. Miss Head confessed in court that she lives in the building at apt 2B on 6/16/14. She also confessed that she has been in charge since 1989.

Manager: As I mentioned before that she is living inside her husband's apartment in the building I live in. She has her relatives living in the same building and the other building if I am not mistaking. It was her relative who lives in 3A (maybe cousin), told me about that they kicked out the child of the shareholder who live next to me at apt 2C, after the Board called police on me January 3, 2014. I was under suspicion about that before because the names of the people who live in the apartment are not registered under their names when I did some investigations. I found out later on about the others as well after that relative told me about that. I did research online and find out that there are four out of ten apartments in both buildings are not registered under the names of the people who inhabited them. The people who their names are registered for the apartments are not even shareholders. Even the new super's name is not registered in the apartment that he lives in. No wonder the person whom I called at the Public sector, told me that he knew about the buildings a long time, during the time I was in court with the Board for the HP-action cases. I do not know if the manager has a decent job. Her daughter has a puppy makes me wondering if they really pay for that puppy with their own money. She has a relative (maybe cousin) who lives with her parents on apt 4C, driving maybe a brand new jeep. The license plate number is (Plate number omitted). That relative used to drive a small Hyundai and change that Hyundai to a new Jeep. I also do not know what type of job that relative has in order to drive such expensive car. Her husband works for the City Agency and drive a car as well. I also wonder if her husband buys the car that he is driving with his own money as well. She also fixed her husband's apartment as well as her relative apartments, makes me wondering where she gets the money to do that as well. I mentioned before that her Husband used to be the president of the buildings. Otherwise, I may be mistaken there. The Manager never comes to court. She came in during the time before I brought the Board on trial. She came in court and left right away. Mr. President and Ms. Manager came to court with Miss Head during the time of the small claim. She did not come to court at all during the time her and the others brought me to court (Holdover Proceeding case). How can she sign a paper for court when she did not show up in court for it? It was only Miss Head and Mr. President showed up in court on 6/4/14 and 6/16/14.

Even the super might have a car. I remembered he told me last year that he got paid $150 or 200 dollars a week to work for the buildings last year (2013). He also told me that he paid every month for the apartment that he lives in.

I send the copies of the tenants who live in the buildings. I sent them before on January 2014. I also send information about the boards as well. No wonder why the board creates their own rules and regulation, to be in their favors. They want everyone to get out of the buildings so that they either rent the apartments or move their relatives to the apartments. Some of the people, who live in the apartments that are not registered under their names, happened to register under the name of the shareholders who used to live in them. The people who control the buildings do not pay anything at all. They happen to be the freeloaders.

Part 5

What goes around comes around Vs. Revenge

I found it dumb and stupid of the board and their lawyer(s) to have Holdover Proceeding case against me. The board and their lawyer(s) actually made the Holdover Proceeding case against me after I sent my responses to them twice. I sent response to the lawyer on January 2014, February 2014, and March 2014. I sent all of the same responses together on May 2014 after I got sick and tired of getting those anonymous envelopes sent by KPS, the Board, and the board's lawyer(s). The board and their lawyer(s) using the same strategy they used during the HP action cases to some degree. I was served by the board one Friday night around the hour of seven at night. I was served late for two reasons. The first reason was that the board stated on the paper that they sent to me anonymously that we owed almost tenth of thousands of dollars. The board sent these anonymous papers in order to try to contradict the response I sent to their lawyer(s). The second reason I was served late was to make sure that I did not have enough time to get a lawyer or not prepared at all. No wonder why I sent response to the board's lawyer(s) and kept record of what I sent to the lawyer(s).

I also received four cards from the Court on the next day, as well as a certified letter sent for my father to pick up at the post office. The board and their lawyer(s) effectively knew that my father had been absent since 2008. The board and their lawyer(s) really like to waste papers for no reason. The board and their lawyer(s) created story to make up stupid case out of. The responses that I sent to the board's lawyer(s) would effectively contradict the story. On the day I came to court, I began to curse the board in front of their lawyer in the hallway at lower tone of voice. I was talking with a Caucasian male who suffered almost the same problem I did, before the board and their lawyer came in. It was the male Caucasian who told me that to hush while I explained my situation to him, and while the board and their lawyer happened to appear all of the sudden. I even point my finger to show the Caucasian male the board.

When it was time to get to the courtroom after spending few minutes sitting down, the board's lawyer tried the same strategy that he did on the second HP action case, on the day I brought the board on trial. This time the board's lawyer did not give me paper on the spot to read in few minutes before I saw the Judge. This time board's lawyer said what he had to say to me verbally. The board' lawyer called my name out loud, just like he did on the HP action case. He brought me outside and said that the landlord did not want me in the apartment, I must leave. I responded by saying that that there was no landlord. I added I by saying to the lawyer "f*** you". The first Judge who held the case before trial heard the conversation that took place at the entrance of the courtroom, asking us out loud to move far away from the entrance. When it was time for me to face the Judge, the board's lawyer played pretentious while I mentioned about the HP action cases. The board's lawyer was under pretentious while having smile on his face. When I showed the Judge the HP action papers I received by the Judges, who held the HP action cases, the board's lawyer whipped the smile off his face.

I told the Judge that about the person's name on the card was my father's name. it started to become a problem for the board and their lawyer when the Judge found out from me that my father had been absent since 2008. The Judge wanted to close case before the Judge found out about my father's absence because the case that the board and their lawyer had against me was lame and fake names had been used on the case. It was the board and their lawyer who wanted to go on trial. The Judge found that the board and their lawyer committed big offense because it was illegal for them to bring a person in court when the person has been absent. The Judge asked me if I sent response, as well as stated on the cards that I received from the court to have my response prepared on the day of the court. These cards happened to be the only thing I did not send to Authority, the Public sector, and Private sector. The Judge collected the first response from instead of all the responses and the envelopes that the board sent to me. The rest of the response collected in court on the day of the trial along with the envelopes that the board sent to me. These documents had been used as evidence and exhibits on the trial of the Holdover Proceeding case. The board's lawyer knew that he was in real trouble because he thought that I would not come to court with my responses. No wonder why the board's lawyer and the board did not give their response to the Judge when the Judge asked them for their response before trial. The lawyer was talking to the president in the hallway after the Judge said that everyone must be there for trial. I heard the lawyer said to the president about that this time the president had to come in, on the hallway, out of the courtroom. The lawyer was unable to sit down because the lawyer looked like he was in a little shock.

On the day of the trial, I met with this Haitian lady. She was may have been in her mid-fifty's. She explained to me about what she had to go through with the landlord of her building. She even told me about the damages in her apartment and the landlord knew about these damages. She even told me that the landlord always changed lawyers every time she came to court. She told me that her landlord probably changed lawyers five times. When she approached the Judge, she unable to understand what the Judge said to her. The Judge even asked her if she needed an interpreter. The lady and I met again miraculously on the day I came to do the appeal the way it should be done. We were talking again about the same issues, when she approached the Court Officer, along with the Interpreter. The Court Officer wanted to find out what the landlord said to her outside of the court. The Haitian lady said that her landlord said not to worry about anything that happened in court. She seemed to believe everything the landlord said to her. However, she wanted to leave the apartment anyway due to the problems that the apartment suffered from.

She even showed me some pictures that she took in the apartment as prove and evidence of the damages. One of the pictures had to do about something that looked like human's remaining in the toilet and unable to flush. She said to the Interpreter and the Court Officer that the landlord found ways to dirt her name online in order to prevent her from getting any apartments throughout the City. She added that it was a relative of her who told her after finding out her name in some sort of list online. The Court Officer while the Interpreter interpreted to her in Creole that the landlord said she must paid twenty dollars on the spot. She did not know why she had to pay all of this money. Therefore, the Court Officer told her that she must put something in writing and came back with it. I would like to help that poor lady despite I had to deal with the illegal eviction that took place against me. The Court would not allow that to happen because the Housing situation is a situation that should taking care of individually. It would be like some kind of invasion of privacy if I helped this poor Haitian woman. My heart was deeply hurt and ache for that poor Haitian woman who was victimized by her landlord due to language barrier and left on her own to deal with the problem. I could have been in the same problem as her if I did not keep record of what had been going on in court and outside of court. I could have been in the same problem as her if I did not know how to speak, read, write, understand English, as well as knowing what is going on around me.

That was almost the same strategy and tactic the board in the buildings I lived in tried to use on me during the HP action case. No wonder I did not go to the ridiculous, useless, and worthless private meeting that should be held by the board and the lady at the Private sector, after I sent response to their lawyer about all the lies, false allegations, and contradiction the board and their lawyer(s) sent to me. I wondered what they would say to me after they were the one created the mess in the first place. The lady at the Private sector sent an email to me on the second time concerning about the private meeting. I received that email probably on the eve of returning to court for the second HP action case. I also wondered what the board and the lady at the Private sector would tell me. They probably told me that do not worry about everything, tell the court that the apartment had been fixed. Otherwise, the board and the lady at UHAB probably wanted to threat by scaring me in any possible way to prevent me from going to court. I do not forget what the lady at the Private sector told me on the second meeting I had with her, when I told her that the first Judge from the second HP action told me about sending response to the board's lawyer. She was the one who told me that the Judge was wrong. Therefore that was what the board and the lady at the Private sector had been doing since the HP action cases until on the day I was evicted illegally.

The problem with the secret meeting was how I can trust the board and the lady at the Private sector about what they would tell me. It was the board who actually crossed the line by putting me through pain since they damage the bathroom floor I leveled. The Haitian lady was not the only one who got hurt by her landlord in court. I saw few people got hurt by their landlords while I was in court during the HP action cases. I saw this lady said to a lawyer that she would post him on Facebook after she discovered what the lawyer had been doing. All the lawyer did was laugh out loud at her. I saw this took place on the day I came probably on the trial of the second HP action case. The Judge was there witness everything and did not say or do anything.

I decided to further my research about the housing issues in general, as well as decided to talk to people about the issues and problems surrounding housing court in Brooklyn. Before I got to this part there were few stories I wanted to include here. It was on March or April 2013, few months before the damage done on the bathroom floor occurred, I used to work in a family shelter in Queens at the end of January 2013. One of the clients who were just came in the shelter, told me one day that he and his wife were evicted from the two bedrooms apartment they were living, after he complained and brought the landlord in court over a problem that happened in the apartment. He told me that he had a lawyer to represent him. However, his lawyer had turned against him in court. He added that his lawyer ended up being on the side of the landlord's lawyer to evict him from the apartment. He and his wife happened to have a son who happened to be in the elementary school. The client happened to be about mid-fifties or early sixties. The same may apply to his wife. He also added that he had been living in the apartment for more than six years and found it unfair for him to get evicted, as well as everything that happened to him in court was strange, unclear, and overwhelming. The client and his wife happened may come from the Middle East or Asia, particularly in India.

However, the client was not the only one who suffered from eviction and other problems in the shelter. I saw some clients who did not appreciate what happened to them which led them to come to the shelter. Some of these clients did not want to live in shelter because of the sign of disgrace and disrespectful for them to be there in the first place. Some of them complained about the shelter system because the shelter bureau that they went to, stressed them not to live in the shelter. One of the problems contributed to that was the "eligibility process" that every shelter recipients or clients had to go through. I saw new faces coming to that shelter almost every two to three weeks during the six months I spent working in the shelter. I saw few people went to that eligibility and ineligible process more than four times a day or a week. Some of the clients were unable to go to work when they had to deal with the ineligibility process. They should found out about the cause of their ineligibility before the deadline from their case workers. I found out that women were more likely to have the problem of ineligibility more than men.

I did universal search about the housing situation, particularly about the holdover proceeding case. I did not do research about that during the time I was served by the board and their lawyer(s). I did not know the meaning of holdover proceeding until I received the cards from the court about there was a holdover proceeding case against me and my mother. The only thing I did research about was the anonymous envelopes that the board and their lawyer(s) sent to me about "John Doe and Jane Doe". I sent response to KPS and G***** & L*** PLLC concerning about "John Doe and Jane Doe". I wondered if "John Doe and Jane Doe" really falls in the category of holdover proceeding. I done research about holdover proceeding by reading the same sources I found in the websites in a month and half after the illegal eviction took place, until the end of the year 2015. I found that the landlord cannot do holdover proceeding while wanted to claim money on rent on top of that. The landlord had to choose one choice out of the two choices, not both at the same time. The cards I received by the Court explained it all. The board and their lawyer(s) chose to do both. The board and their lawyer(s) had holdover proceeding against me, meanwhile trying to claim money on top of that invisibly under the holdover proceeding. Therefore, the board and their lawyer(s) trapped with both of them. The board and their lawyer(s) also trapped by turning the HDFC Co-Op into landlord and Corporation. Otherwise the board and their lawyer(s) must bring the landlord in court if there was a landlord. The president testified that HDFC is the landlord.

The board already went against the rules and regulations of the HDFC Co-Op by acting as landlord and creating their laws. The board even brought a proprietary lease during the trial of the holdover proceeding that was about seven pages. However, the proprietary lease may not have it uses in HDFC Co-Op. The TIL never mentioned anything about proprietary lease, but only about the Bylaws as I mentioned before. My father seemed to never receive proprietary lease before and/or after the buildings turned into Co-Op as I mentioned before. My father may never receive the Bylaws as well. Since the board and their lawyer(s) putted on the first, second, and third envelope that they sent to me during the HP action cases, turned out to be a big foul for them. I decided to surf on the internet and download a proprietary lease which turned out to be useless, meaningless, and worthless. I knew about that after I was evicted. It was still going to be the board and their lawyer(s) problems because it was the board responsibility to give us such documents. Therefore the board and their lawyer(s) tried to use proprietary lease and other documents against me by trying to scare me from moving forward with HP action cases.

The same website I went to get information about the holdover proceeding case stated that the holdover proceeding case is very serious and complicated matter because it has to do about situations far deeper than money. The website stated that landlords are more likely would win because they have lawyers represent them. The tenants are more likely to lose because the tenants do not have lawyers to represent them, as well as unable to afford to pay for lawyers. However, the source did not give enough details about why this happened. Some of the reasons this happened, was that some of tenants may suffer from language barrier. These tenants would effectively have trouble to deal with what happened in court, as well as trouble to understand what happened on their cases. The Haitian lady was an example of that, as well as other Haitians and non-Haitians who effectively suffered from the language barrier problem. The Haitian lady was unable to understand what the Judge said to her, as well as unable to understand what the landlord had done to her. I found that Haitians happened to be one of the nations who happened to face more abuse in Housing Court. Someone recently told me that there was this Haitian woman who was evicted with her new born child (one weekend of October 2016) while we were talking about what happened in Haiti and in the U.S. Therefore, the court would evict anyone who is effectively physically disabled.

A friend of the relative of my mother's friend, where we took private shelter after the illegal eviction took place, said that Haitians faced more abused in Housing Court after I explained to him about what happened to us. However, the source was not entirely right about tenants lose their cases if they did not have lawyers to defend them. Remember the story about the shelter recipient said that his lawyer turned against him in court, and evicted from his apartment. What about tenants who understand English? These tenants may not even understand what is going on in court even though these tenants may able to read, write, and speak English. That happened because of the confusion that occur in court both verbally and on papers. There were few people I talked to about the housing situation and what had been going in court. I talked to these people, not only to know about their awareness, but also about found out if they had been in the Housing Court in downtown Brooklyn. Two out of the few I talked to about the housing situation told me what I wanted to hear from them. They also give more information as well.

One of them happened to be a co-worker. We worked in the same building for the same client as security officer. However, I worked in the building just to complete my training. It was around the time I was court on the HP action case. The co-worker was about my father's age, and I did not know if he was doing paralegal on the side. He was the one who told me about that he took class to certify as paralegal. He told me that he went in court to testify against people who did not pay anything for twenty, thirty years. He was shocked when I explained to him about what the board had been doing in the building(s) I lived, particularly about the identity thief and the name of the CEO who passed away was still in used.

When I got my permanent site, I talked to an employee who came to clean carpet for the client at night. I explained to him about the illegal eviction that took place and was not surprised about that because he was in the same situation with his landlord. He was the one told me about what people who control the buildings reported to the government was different than what they did in private. That concerned about rent that happened illegally which the government may or may not know about. That was the same thing the board in the building(s) I lived did. The board rented few apartments on subletting. That also proved that the board never renewed documents and decided to come to court with the first list that came out in 1988-1989 as current information about the buildings; along with $275 (or $250) on rent stated on the list. The board sent wrong information to HPD and eventually going to cause problem for the Public sector and themselves. All of my findings effectively proved everything. The same employee also told me that he was robbed by a lawyer, since I mentioned that first to him.

The others I spoke to about my situation and being in downtown court in Brooklyn were shocked about what had been going on in the courtroom. Few of these people even told me that Jewish lawyers were more likely caused problems in court. That was what happened to me because the board hired Jewish lawyer(s) to cause problems and wrongdoings in court, and evicted me from the apartment illegally. Few of these people told me that Italian lawyers were better because they knew how to handle Jewish lawyers in court. Few of them also told me that Jewish lawyers know each other and never going against each other. The rest I explained my situation never been in court and unware that they were at war with the people in charge of their buildings. What I explained to them sounded crazy, as well as unable to handle what I said to them. Some I explained about what happened to me, later on went to court and found out what I told them about the housing court in Brooklyn was right. Their reactions toward me were like they saw evil going on in the courtroom. Some of these people I talked to about my situation, majority of them happened to be Haitians. Some of these people told me that their landlords brought them in court for no reason. Their landlords accused them about rent payment when they actually paid their rents and owed nothing on rent.

There was another website I checked talked about the holdover proceeding is a serious case. The landlord must prove why he/she has holdover proceeding against a tenant. If the landlord cannot prove anything, the tenant can use anything against the landlord. If the landlord happened to evict the tenant illegally, the tenant must leave the apartment without arguing with the Marshal. Otherwise the tenant would be in trouble with the Marshal. The landlord had to go in court to bring proof why the tenant had been evicted. The tenant must live the apartment and go to a hotel and kept record of the payments he/she made in the hotel. The information I found on the website was strange for two reasons. The first reason had to do about that the tenant must able to afford to pay for hotel. The website seemed to talk about tenants who are living in middle class, not lower or working class. What is the whole point of keeping records of payment for hotel? I will find it absurd of the court to ask me record of what I pay during the time I evicted. I paid cash on private shelter with no proof of. The court should have been the one to find me a place since the court went along with the eviction, without proof why I should be evicted. New York City happened to suffer from housing and that led to corruption. Some people like to take money or not and they do not want to take responsibility they do not want to take responsibility of the mess they created. The second reason had to do about tenants who live in buildings control by landlords, not Co-Ops. The website did not give details or explanation about tenants who live in Co-Ops facing the same situation.

I checked another website which had something in common about HDFC because this website had to do about people's comments of HDFC. There were things captured my attention from the website for two reasons. The first reason had to do about a broker who gave details about that shareholders in HDFC buildings cannot sell their apartments due to the reason that the bank never gets involve when there are so many renters. Therefore, the bank would never make profit that way. The broker added that good luck to people who were not shareholders, living in the HDFC Co-Ops. The board just let people who are not shareholders, live in apartments under subletting. It was from the broker I knew about the word "subletting". The second reason had to do about few people's comments about the problems and issues that happened in the HDFC buildings were similar to what had been going on in the HDFC buildings I lived. One of the problems and issues had to do about the bills of the buildings came in to their apartments which happened to send to the wrong apartments, ended leaving on the mail box as returning mail. The other problems and issues had to do about some of the board members have more than one apartment in the buildings. That also true because the manager had more than one apartment in both buildings. No wonder why the board kept everything about their families living in the buildings on low profile. No wonder why not everyone know everybody's full names, except the list of the names that the board placed on the small boxes, about ten feet high, which everyone may forget about if they do not pay attention about them. All the names on the list only had the first letter of the first names and the last names. Some of the last names were effectively misspelling on purpose so that the board can bring people in court saying that they owed money or live in the apartments illegally. The first names can effectively misspelling on purpose as well. My father's first name and last name had been misspelled by the board on purpose, particularly by the president since he was the one who caused more problems. The board effectively knew how my father's full name spells. How that can be a mistake about misspelling my father's name improperly? No wonder why my father told me to make copies of the money orders along with his name on them before I gave the money to the head, before I received the receipts. However, we may not be the only one suffered from the misspelling of full names.

I checked two more websites during the time I was evicted from the apartment illegally and found out about two matters. The first matter had to do about some people who in charge of buildings spent millions of dollars in court every year on lawyers trying to destroy the law that protected the tenants. A lot of people in the working class would be in serious trouble, particularly African American who faced more problems in the Housing Court. The second matter had to do about that the landlords would never give up fighting in court, as well as give up that easy. I found this part in coincidence to the issues and problems I had to deal with the board in the Co-Op I live. The board and their lawyers tried to do whatever necessary to play dirty in court was a way to prove that they would not gave up that easily. No wonder why I said that the Housing issues and problems would get worse.

There were few more websites I checked during the time I was evicted. The website talked about the rules and regulations that were implemented to prevent lawyers do get involved in any illegal activities with their clients. It was illegal for a lawyer to commit perjury in court. Lawyers must do their works base on ethics. It was also illegal for a lawyer to give a client wrong definition of the court papers or documents. That was what I to deal with when I was evicted illegally. I was robbed by a lawyer and used me as a scapegoat (patsy) because he gave wrong definition of the court paper. The lawyer blamed me by saying that I was the one who tried to cancel the Judge's decision and advised me not to do so. He charged one thousand seven hundred dollars and gave me a shitty and worthless appeal when I asked him to give me back my money. The shitty and worthless appeal he gave almost jeopardized everything for me. There are more in details about what happened in part six. As for the Judges, the Judges should never choose side. The Judges should never choose side with lawyers even though they know these lawyers because that would affect everything that happen in court due to favoritism.

There was another website I checked about landlord in Co-Ops. The website stated that some landlords were not completely gone away because these landlords happened to be the ones who controlled these Co-Ops invisibly. No wonder why the person I chose on the list that the court gave me to choose from, told me that the people in charge the buildings happened to be the landlords. It was evident that the board acting as landlord. I found strange of them unable to bring the landlord in court. Otherwise the board was a bunch of cowards who afraid to testify in court that they were the landlords. No wonder why I said the board control by bunch of dumb and stupid people on the response that collected in court before the trial of the holdover proceeding case. The landlord problem became more of the problem for the board because the landlord supposed to be a person, not an object that one could not see. Another problem that the board faced is to use the Co-Ops as Corporation. I remembered the president told me that HDFC is a corporation, before I went to court to file for HP action. It seemed to me that the word corporation begins to lose its meaning there. Otherwise the board wanted to represent everything at ones due to the power and privileges that they bring to them. What about HDFC as a non-profit organization? It was also dumb and stupid of the board's lawyer(s) to represent the board in court on these problems that they knew about. Otherwise, greedy for money got the best of the lawyer(s) to represent the board without thinking that they would go down with their clients. I would not be surprised if these lawyers or law firm would be around and continued doing all the wrongdoings that they have done to me and everyone else before and after me, and not having these lawyers licenses revoked. This may not happen because of about the Benjamin. I would not be surprised that if the board staying in their apartments and continue not paying their fair share.

There were two sets of problems that the board and their lawyer(s) faced on the trial of the holdover proceeding. The first sets of problems were that the board and their lawyers committed to us on the HP action cases and the Small Claim case. These set of problems were prejudice, discrimination, disrespectful, identity theft, perjury, scam, harassment, and attempted to kick us out by calling the police on us twice. All of these wrongdoings that the board and their lawyer(s) committed toward us were done by injustice and inhuman. The other sets of problems that the board had to face had to do about the subletting, the bills of the buildings, anonymous, falsify of documents and information, and behave as landlords. The board and their lawyers had to deal with all of these problems on the holdover proceeding case. The board and their lawyers never brought what I had on the responses the first Judge collected from me, before the trial of the Holdover Proceeding case. The response that the court collected from me had been used as ways that there were a lot of clarities, grounds, and focus on the trial. The responses that the court collected from me had been used to contradict and destroy everything that board and their lawyer(s) would do on trial of the holdover proceeding. The responses that the court collected from had been used as a way to prevent the board and their lawyer(s) to create confusion in court.

The board and their lawyer(s) had nothing against me. The board and their lawyers had the guts and nerves trying to around of what I had on my response without showing proof of them. The board and their lawyer(s) ended bring documents that I did not ask them to bring in court. These few documents that the board and their lawyer(s) brought in court would eventually further the problem for them and the buildings. One of these documents had to do about the first list that came out during 1988-1989 as current information about the buildings, as I mentioned before. The board's families would eventually affect the most about these documents because their names may not include on the list. The president was effectively affected by the list because his name was not on the list. He testified against himself in court saying that he lived in an apartment that was not under his name as shareholder. There was no proof of him on documents stated that he was a shareholder. The manager seemed to be in the same problem as well because the apartment that she lives may not be on documents stated that she lives in the apartment. That apartment happened to be on the name of the shareholder who was affected by the July 2010 fire. The shareholder transferred to the other building and board never kept any record of her transferred to the other building. The chief may suffer as well because the apartment seemed to be under her husband's name. The apartment may remain under her husband's since her husband passed away. Therefore that had been proving that the board did not keep records of the buildings as well as updated these records. The shareholder who was affected by the July 2010 fire told me that the board also blamed the CEO/Chair who passed away for not keeping records of the buildings. The shareholder also added that the CEO's son may throw all of these documents away when the board accused them of using the buildings finance for private gain and kicked him out of the buildings.

I have been both predictable and unpredictable toward the board and their lawyer(s). I had been predictable about the response that I sent to the board's lawyer(s). I was unpredictable about my findings and the TIL. I came with copies of the envelopes that the board's lawyer(s) sent to me during the HP action cases while I took stand. I was included briefly about what had been going on the HP action case, when I took stand on the trial of the holdover proceeding. The court (referred to the Judge) did not collect the copies of these envelopes from as evidence and exhibits on the trial of the holdover proceeding. The court did not even collect the copies of my citizenship, mother's, and my father's as evidence or exhibit. The Judge looked at them and gave them back to me. The Judge did not even collect the fake Bylaws that the board gave me as evidence and exhibit, even though the Bylaws had been included on the response collected in court, as well as recorded in court what I said about the Bylaws. The experience I had in court was that I did not know how the trial was going to handle. I mentioned earlier about being a petitioner or defendant goes vice versa to some degree. I was more a defendant and less of petitioner because I have all the leverage on the board and their lawyer(s). The board happened to be petitioners who brought me in court, ended up placing in defensive mode, had to go on stand first due to my responses. It was also suicide of the board and their lawyer(s) to bring me in court when I had everything at my disposal to bring them down, as well as put them in serious problems and troubles.

One of the bigger problems that the board suffered was to lie under oath about the money that the board said we owed and never brought proof in court about that. Another lied had to about that the president never proved how he became president when it was my turned to ask him question about that. The only thing that the board did as truth and proof was to come to testify against themselves about living in their apartments because I was forced them to tell the truth about that; due to the fact that they said they did not live in their apartments, as well as tried to set me up with Miss Head's apartment, which led the board changing information about the way I filed for the HP action cases. That also include briefly on the response that the court collected from me on the holdover proceeding case. The only person never showed up in court was Miss Manager. The board did not aware that their lawyer(s) were gave them up in court and tried to save themselves from the problem they helped their clients created in the first place. I would not allow the board and their lawyer(s) to make mess out of the holdover proceeding case just like they did on the HP action cases and small claim case. Therefore, I used everything that the board and their lawyer(s) did on the previous cases against the board and their lawyer(s). I was also out to get the board's lawyer(s) because the lawyer(s) happened to be my primary targets since the HP action cases. The board's lawyer(s) happened to be the main contributors to what had been going in court and to us and the buildings. I found that there is nothing sweeter than trapping a lawyer with his/her client.

"One weekend on July 2016, I play the audio transcripts that the court sent to me about the trial of the holdover proceeding. There was something I discovered what the board's lawyer said at the conclusion of the holdover proceeding's trial. He said to the Judge that he did not receive anything from me. What kind of lawyer would represent a client in court without knowing what is going on in the case? The board's lawyer also said to the Judge that he would like to get back all of the documents that his clients gave in court as evidence and exhibits. The board's lawyer did not want the court to make copies of all of these documents. I found it absurd of the board and their lawyer(s) to bring me in court after they deprive me from my sleep and rest three times during the holdover proceeding case. The lawyer found out that he was trapped along with his clients because he witnessed some of what I sent to the law firm, as well as witnessed everything in court during the trial. I found it absurd of the lawyer to make ridiculous case against me by saying on paper that the lawyer's fees were a false allegation I had against him. He also said that because I asked the Judge to provide me with a paper in order to protect me from the lawyer's fees at the end of the trial of the holdover proceeding case. The proof that I had against the lawyer was that he had to commit perjury, identity theft, and falsify information and documents in order to get pay. The lawyer and his clients did not take what the Judge wrote as decision on the paper that the Judge gave his clients and me on the first HP action case into account. The same lawyer said on my face that I would pay his fees after found out he trapped with his client on the small claim case. The lawyer found out that there was no way out of anything, but only further the problem to himself and his law firm, just like his clients further the problem that they created to themselves. Another proof I

have was on the receipts. The receipt sent as proof to the lawyer before I went to court before the holdover proceeding case took effect. The lawyer also witnessed what I sent to him as proof collected in court as evidence and exhibit on the trial of the holdover proceeding. The reason why the board's lawyer continued denied that he did not receive anything from was that the anonymous that he played allowed him to get away with anything. The lawyer used the law firm as corporation to take all the blame for his wrongdoings in order to protect himself from having his license revoked and ruin his reputation. No wonder why the envelopes that these lawyers sent to me did not have any name on them. The law firm was not a legit law firm because the names of the lawyers must be included on the envelopes sent by the law firm. However, the first lawyer who represented the board from all of the cases happened to be more of a lawyer. I wonder how much these lawyers charge the board to represent the board on the holdover proceeding case, particularly the trial of the holdover proceeding."

I also made sure that the board and their lawyer(s) did not use anything as excuses by saying that they made mistakes. I said that for two reasons. The first reason had to do about the lady who got affected by the fire in July 5, 2010 told me that the board used things as excused to get away with the wrongdoings that they committed towards her. The board knew effectively they wanted to kick her out of the apartment and rented the apartment on subletting. The second reason had to do about the prisoner dilemma that may happen in court before the trial. I did not know what the board and their lawyer(s) reported to court before the trial of the holdover proceeding. The board and their lawyer(s) effectively knew that they wanted to evict us illegally from the apartment due to gentrification and subletting. I did what I could to have the board and their lawyer(s) got caught on their own predicaments, troubles, and problems. The tenant who was affected by the July 2010 fire had a lawyer to help her out after the fire. However, her lawyer did not do anything to help solving the whole problems that the buildings suffered, but only charged her a lot of money just to patch things up in court for her.

It was the same lawyer that the tenant told me to go to see when I was evicted illegally which stole my money. The lawyer knew effectively that he could not do anything about my case because the Judge already made his decision. The lawyer decided to give me the wrong definition of the court paper, and later on blamed me by saying that I was the one who tried to cancel the Judge's decision, when I asked him to give me back my money. I was under suspicion that the lawyer knew his client would get affected by what the Judge wrote on the second paper. I was also under suspicion that the lawyer did not tell me that the board's lawyer and the board went against the Judge's decision. I was also under suspicion that the lawyer probably made a deal with the board's lawyer(s), without his client knew about that during the time he held his client's case. However, the lawyer was not the only one gave me the wrong definition of the court paper or document, as well as blaming me for not doing anything about the situation in court. There was a woman I approached on the second floor where to file for HP action, told me it was I who told the Judge to get me out of the apartment, after she read the Judge's decision.

There was another lawyer that my oldest sister, my mother and I went to see after the illegal eviction took place, few days later after I robbed by the first lawyer. The second lawyer told me almost the same thing that the first lawyer told me about not doing anything about the problem. The second lawyer also gave me the wrong definition of the court paper. The other lawyer even wanted to charge me almost the same fees the first lawyer charged me to give me another shitty and worthless appeal. The second lawyer even made it an obligation to pay one hundred dollars fees for about fifteen minutes of visit he spent on the useless and worthless information he gave me about my case. The two lawyers, particularly the one who stole my money, wanted to charge me about what the court knew, as well as ignored my responses and exhibits the Judge collected in court from me. The first lawyer did charge me for what the court knew. The first lawyer ended steal what the court knew and charged me for it.

The biggest problem that contributed to the buildings had to do about the board and their lawyer went against the Judge's decision. That also counted of them being disrespectful toward the Judge and the court system. The board and their lawyer(s) thought they could do whatever they want regardless they found guilty of all the wrongdoings they had committed. The board and lawyers could not prove anything in court and they trapped in the abyss of their problems, troubles, and predicaments that they putted themselves into before and after the trial. I did what I could to make sure that the board and their lawyer(s) could never get away with anything. There was one person out of few people who read the Judge's decision along with the response that the court collected, understand deeply about what happened on the housing situation, during the time I was evicted illegally; about few months later. That person happened to tell me that I got these bastards. That person also told me that the people in charge of the buildings should find me a place to live, since they were the ones who evicted me illegally. That person even went to someone who specialized in court with the court paper I gave her to get more information out of everything for me. The rest of the few seemed to be confused about what the Judge wrote on the Judge's decision. They even told me that I lost the case without proving to me on the Judge's decision where. No wonder why some people do not know a difference between cases that have been "granted" or" denied" on the court papers.

There were two things I found out that were illegal for lawyers to do to their clients. The first thing was that it is illegal for lawyers to take money or charge their clients when the court cases are not over. I did not know if there was such law. I discovered about that law through one of the building security where I used to work at night. He was my countryman. I explained to him about the housing situation I had been through, as well as I was robbed by a lawyer. The building security was the one who told me that it was illegal for a lawyer to take money from a client when the case was not solved yet. The building security also told me that his landlord hired the law firm that the board in the building I lived to represent his landlord, when I showed him the court papers sent by the board's lawyer(s). The same building guard also told that he suffered from mice problems in his apartment, as well as heating problem. The same building security also told me that it was serious problem for me that I did not have a place to live. The building security was right about that. He was the only person who told me about the seriousness of my condition than the other people. The other few people told me that to forget about the apartment and found another apartment. They failed to pay attention deeply that the whole city had been suffered from apartment problems or housing for four reasons. The first reason had to do about the scarcity for apartments due to supply and demand. The population of New York City which over populated leading to high demand to apartments while the supply of that had been stagnated. The second reason had to do about prejudice, discrimination, and injustice, toward African Americans to find apartments in the city. The third reason had to do about income. Majority of people could not afford to have forty to sixty percent of their income went on rent. Majority of people in New York City have income range from 15000-25000 a year. The fourth reason had to do about many people have been dislocated in the city due illegal eviction and/or not that had been taken place. I could get an apartment already if it was easy to find one. Another building security who happened to be my countryman told me not to go to see a lawyer and kept my money in my pocket when I explained to him about the illegal eviction that took place. It was the same morning before I went to see the lawyer for the first time after work that morning. I did take the building security's word or advice into account and consideration. I left vulnerable and confused about what happened to me because it was unclear and uncertain what to do next after the illegal eviction that took place. I did not know if it was illegal for a lawyer to give a client a wrong definition of the court paper and gave the client a shitty and worthless appeal.

It was by luck I got to a point that the appeal done properly after the court messed up by sending me to legal aid; after the court discovered about the useless and worthless appeal without asking me where the appeal came from. The court gave me a list that had the addresses of all legal aid offices in Brooklyn. I went to one of the legal aid offices located not far away from the court. The legal aid ended up sending me back to court after they found out about the court case was complex, as well as found out about my response that the court collected from me. They told me that was not what they took care of in their office. The legal aid told me that to go to the floor I should go in court, to start the appeal, after I spent and wasted two weeks of my time. It was not until almost the last day of October 2014 the appeal done properly. I was mad and pissed off about what I had to go through with the court and decided to report to the Judge who handled the trial of the holdover proceeding case about what I had to through; and the Judge and the court must held responsible and accountable for what I had to go through to some degree, by sending a letter to the Judge. I also let the Judge knew about the apartment had been renting under our names on subletting and notified the gentleman at the Public sector and the lady at the Private sector about that as well. I also send report to Authority about everything.

The second letter I sent to the Judge about a year after the illegal eviction took place because I was concerned about the appeal. I did not send the second letter to the Justice Department because of the workload I had to do to send the second letter to the Justice department. The second letter had to do about how long the appeal would take because no one told me how long the appeal would take, as well as not knowing the status of my appeal. The person I chose from the list could not tell me how long the appeal would take, and never called me back after I left messages for that person. The person I chose from the list told me that the appeal can take longer when I met with her for the first time in December 31, 2014, without some clarity on that. I sent the second letter to the Judge to let the Judge knew how could the court made decision without knowing how long the appeal would take. The second letter I sent to the Judge to let the Judge knew that the court must find me a place to live since I did not know where I was standing on the appeal. The Judge did not even send response to me since I stated that I hope to hear from the Judge about what the court would do with me, after spending almost two years of being homeless. The main reason I sent the letter to the Judge was that I began to get some attitude toward my mother's friend and her daughter about to get us out of their apartment for two reasons. That first reason had to do about they do not want my mother's friend got in trouble with their landlord about us being in their apartment illegally. Otherwise they just acted stupidly because they wanted us to be out. The second reason had to do about the need of physical address to do the appeal. That was an issue I had to deal with to do the appeal. The last remaining of this part sent to the Justice Department. The response the court collected from sent to the gentleman at the Public sector along with the Judge's decisions. I had to send everything to the gentleman at Public sector because he assumed that I was an illiterate man, after the board and the lady at the private sector provided the Public sector with wrong information about what had been going on in court and to us. The gentleman at the Public sector was eager to draw conclusion on something he did not know what was going on into it.

• Sent to Authority
• Sent to the gentleman at the Public sector

Answer one collected in court before trial

My name omitted

Note: address omitted for the purpose of the book

1/17/14

Dear sir or madam

I send you this letter in response of your letter to me and my father. There is one thing I want you to know about the HP action. I went to court with the board after the super damaged my bathroom floor on July 2nd, 2013. I spoke with the board (**boards name omitted**) many times before I went to court on August because they do not want to fix the damage. I want you to know that I built the bathroom floor with my money, May 2012. I want you to know that I went to court to have the first HP action done without having inspector come to the apartment, just to save the board from trouble. The board and the board's lawyer came to court and accused me of trying to sue HDFC, that is why I did not have inspector to come and the apartment, and I am not the shareholder. They both never said that I am the son of the shareholder and the wife of the shareholder is there. The shareholder (**My father**) let me (**my name omitted**) and my mother (**name omitted**) responsible for the apartment during his absence, and the board knew about his absent. My father absence had to do about his retirement from work, and some illness he had to deal with, as well as other businesses he has to deal with back in his home country. I was trying to save the board from the HP action if they did not come to court and lied about everything. I had a second HP action done and had inspector to come in the apartment. I want you to know that I got advice from a lawyer. The lawyer told me what my responsibilities are in a CO-OP when I came to court to have the first HP action done. He told me my responsibilities are to buy materials to put on the floor. The lawyer also said to me that the internal physical structure of the apartment is the board or landlord responsibility, as well as the board or landlord is responsible for the mess done by the super. Even the super said that the board is responsible for his mess, when I confronted him on July 17, 2013. It was the president, told me I can go to court against the super, as well as gives me the super's full name. The board even lied by saying that they are not in charge on the HP action papers sent to me by their lawyer. The board even lied about that I live in 2B. I sent their lawyer response when the first judge for the second HP action told me that I must sent response at what the board's lawyer would send me, and I have the right to disagree at what the lawyer would sent me. The board's lawyer sent me almost the same paper that he sent me for the first HP action and second HP action. Both papers had lies and false allegations against me. I sent my response back to the board's lawyer on the false allegations and lies, as well as sent my proposal because I know for facts that the board does not want to do anything when it comes to fix and do good work in the apartment. None of what the board and their lawyer put on paper represented in court, in front of the Judges. I also want you to know that I spoke with another lawyer while I had filed the second HP action. The lawyer told me that it does not matter if you live in a CO-OP, you must get maintenance if I pay for maintenance every month. The lawyer said to me that the rent that I pay every month is the maintenance. The lawyer asked me if my father and I share the responsibility. I responded to him, yes.

When I came back to court to see a second Judge, the board's lawyer gave me a paper five to ten minutes before I saw the judge. They claim that I want to have the apartment fix because it is there for sale, and the board would charge my father for maintenance. That was not what supposed to happen. I said to the judge that we are not going to sell the apartment. I said to the judge that I have the By Law, showed my responsibility. I said to the judge that I saw contradiction at what the board's lawyer sent me. I said to the judge that I sent the board's lawyer something. The board's lawyer lied in front of the judge by saying that he did not receive anything from me. The Judge told me to come back with everything I had for part B (trial). When I came back to court for trial, the board changed lawyer and tried to come up with new things. The board was surprised when they saw that they would face the same Judge for the trial. They kept lying about sending people to fix the apartment. The new lawyer even mentioned to the Judge about I am not the shareholder and I could not be in court. The Judge said to the lawyer that I am in court represent my father and there is nothing wrong with that and not being a shareholder was totally unrelated to the HP action case. I let the Judge knew that the same people who are in charge of the buildings are the board of director, the board, and shareholders (even though some of them may not be a shareholder, as well as not paying their fair share). I also let the Judge knew that the fiduciary responsibility of the board is to take care of their shareholders. I also let the Judge knew that I called HPD and someone who works at HPD told me that the internal physical structure of the apartment is the board responsibilities, not the shareholder. They came with the proprietary least that looks so fake, and the Bylaws was excluded. I let the board's lawyer to ask the board about how many pages the Bylaws is. There was no respond from the board and the lawyer. I also said to the board's lawyer that I had a proprietary least in my bag, let's compared them. There was nothing done about that as well. I insisted that what the board brought to court is the Bylaws, and the Judge said lets go to trial. I took summon and the judge asked to show what I have, not too much because no one had time for too much. I had a lot to show in court, but I could not do so after what the judge told me. I said to the judge I withdraw from everything. The proprietary least did not even had it used in court for the HP action. I had been trying to negotiate with the board in court, they just too stubborn about that. It is the board should be held responsible for everything that happened in court. I did not want things to get that far. The board has been control by bunch of people who are careless, oppressive, discriminatory, prejudice, arrogant, and ignorant. They are the one who gave me the Bylaws before I went to court, after the super tried to charge me on bogus charges and claimed that the Bylaws said it. He even charged me on bogus charges to fix the toilette. He damaged the floor I built in May 2012. Does it said in the Bylaws or Proprietary least that the Board and the Corporation would never be held responsible and accountable for damaging a shareholder private property.

I send you this letter to let you know that the board cannot kick anyone out of their apartments. They must bring me to court for that, to prove the reason why I should get kick out. The board does not have this kind of absolute and relative right and power to do such things. The board pretends that they do not leave in the buildings. The board must bring me to court to explain to the judge why we have to pay $ 4231. 25 dollars for maintenance we never get, as well as we never get for more than 27 years, since we have been living in the apartment. They must also bring the Bylaws, Proprietary least, stock certificate, and other documents to court for analysis and investigation. I also have the proprietary least and more documents to compare with what the board has. The board must explain to the court the purpose of the stock certificate. Is the stock certificate legit, real, and approve by the government. The stock certificate becomes an issue when I have to deal with the bathroom floor issue and situation. If they have record of the stock certificates for everyone in both buildings, they must provide records of them, particularly for **their apartments.** The apartment I live in has been my primary address for more than 14 years. The board must prove who vote them, particularly the president. Having this kind of "**John Doe and Jane Doe**" against me is foolish, stupid, and dumb of the board. That "**John Doe and Jane Doe**" should be used against the board since they said on court paper that they do not leave in the Buildings, as well as not in charge of the buildings. HPD and the government know I live in the apartment. The assistant at UHAB knew about me when I explained to her about the reason why my father is absent. She told me that is not a problem for us to pay the rent under my father's name. What the board and their lawyers (**G***** and L****) send me is illegal and can be used against them in court of law. You need to go to the downtown court in Brooklyn and ask record for the HP action number index: omitted and omitted. Compare them to see the difference on how I have them done. The board also called police on me on December 31, 2013 and January 3, 2014 trying to get me in trouble, particularly on January 3, 2014. That can also be used against them in court of law. The board is just bunch of people only send paper and does not want to talk to anyone, as well as afraid of confrontation. I send response to these addresses below because the letter that sent to me has been prepared and sent from one address **(KPS)** and prepare by the board and their lawyer to another address (**G***** & L*** PLLC**).

Sincerely

My name omitted

Note: Addresses of the other places are omitted for the purpose of the book.

Answer two collected in court during the trial

G***** & L***, PLLC

Note: address omitted of the purpose of the book.

3/20/14

To G*****& L***, PLLC

I send you copies of the same documents that I sent to you in the middle of January 2014 when you and your clients (Mr. President, Miss Manager, and Miss Head) try to get me kicked out illegally in my father's apartment. I also include the receipt that Mr. President charges me for lawyer's fees. They have to come to court on April 10, 2014(small claim) explaining to the Judge about these illegal fees. They also called police for me on December 31, 2013 and January 3, 2014 trying to have me getting kick out of my father's apartment and claimed that the Proprietary Least said that they do not want to accept money orders from us for the apartment anymore. They returned the money order that I paid for the apartment on January 2014, along with two letters. One of the letters has to do about false accusation against my mother. The other letter has to do about nothing, but stupidity they put in it. Let them know I still make payments for the apartment. We are not going to be held responsible if the money orders expired. They also have to explain why the head's last name has been changed into another last name. As I said on the response that I sent to you in the middle of January 2014, that your clients have to bring the **Proprietary Least,** to prove where it is stated on the **Proprietary Least** that the corporation would not be held responsible and accountable for damaging a shareholder's property. Your clients also have to bring the **Bylaws** and stated how many pages the **Bylaws** is.

Sincerely

My name omitted

Note: address omitted for the purpose if the book.

Answer three collected in court during the trial

G***** & L***, PLLC

Note: Address omitted for the purpose of the book

4/22/14

To G*****& L***

I send response of the same letter that my Father (**shareholder**) and I (**my name omitted**) received many times in January 2014. It seems to me that KPS and G***** & L*** seem not to understand, as well as listen when to quit. I already sent 47 pages of report to the Justice Department. That report included everything that had been going in court, outside court, court papers that sent to me by G***** & L***, and record of letters that I sent out to G***** & L*** and KPS. I also sent every mail that I receive from your clients to the Justice Department as well. I also sent recordings along with the report. G***** & L***, KPS, and their clients (omitted names) will be held responsible and accountable for their wrongdoings and perjury. I have been warning you all about everything. You all want to keep further the pain and problem.

Sincerely

Name omitted

Name omitted

Note: address is omitted for the purpose of the book.

Name of the gentleman at the Public sector omitted

Position and location omitted

The City Of New York

(Address omitted for the purpose of the book)

7/6/14

Letter to **(name omitted)**

My name is (name omitted), the son of the Shareholder (name omitted), and the Wife of the shareholder, (name omitted). I send this letter in the response of the paper that you sent to let you that we are not going to be held responsible and accountable for the financial problems of the Buildings (address omitted). We have done our share in the buildings for three decades. We never miss out on the rent. The people who cause the problem are the board (**board names omitted**). They also behave as landlords in the buildings. I also want to remind you that it is because of the landlord's problems caused the buildings turn into CO-OP. We are disagreeing with the choice of bringing back landlord in the buildings. The only thing that can happen is that to get rid of the board because the board only cares about themselves and their families. However doing so would raise one problem. That problem would be who wants to inherit the financial mess and problem done by the board. They are shareholders as well, even though they do not pay anything for over 20 years. That is what **the lady at the Private sector** told me when I went to see her in her office, after the super damage the bathroom floor that I built for my parents May 2012. The board knew about the problem and did not want to do anything about the problem. She knows about everything that happens in the buildings, as well knowing about everything the board does. She also agrees at everything the board does. The board owed us about tenth of thousands of dollars in private maintenance for three decades, since we are not the only one that the board owed on private maintenance. I brought them to court and found out that one problem led to all other problems. Some of these problems are the name of the CEO/Chair who passed away since May 2008, is still in used (**name omitted**). The board pretended that they did not leave in the buildings. The location of the Corporation is located at (address omitted) apt 3B, inside the president's apartment, instead at (address omitted) apt 3B. The president became president due to the favoritism done by the head and manager. Some of the apartments in the buildings have been rented by tenants, not shareholders. Few of these apartments are not even registered under the names of the people who live in them. The board also takes the buildings finance to renovate their apartments while they do not fix anyone's apartments, beside theirs and their families and relatives. They even say that the internal physical structure of the apartments are the shareholders responsibility, as well as it is stated in the Bylaws and Proprietary Lease. They even use fake names to represent themselves in court. They even lied in court, as well as committed perjury. The board's lawyer G***** & L*** PLLC and LLP, is also part of the problems. They have been lying in court from the HP actions I filed against them last year (2013), the small claim last year (2013), and until they brought me in court early this June (2014). They brought me in court because they tried to make us paid for their lawyer's fees with high interest on top of that, as well as we owed illegal maintenance fees. They said that we owed in maintenance. They said that we owed about $8000, $9000, or $11000 dollars in maintenance which they cannot prove to be true in court. The board also misspelled my father's first name on purpose, as well as used my first as my last name in court. The board even called police on twice to have me kicking out of the apartment. That was what they do because one of their relatives who live at (address omitted) told me that the board kicked the child of the shareholder who lives next to me out of the apartment. The board raised the rent on shareholders and tenants four to five times already illegally. The board raised the rent by 14% last year. The shareholders are paying over $500 and $600 per month for rent without the light and case bill included. The tenants are paying over $1000 and $1300 per month for rent. The Bylaws and the proprietary lease are fakes because the board created their own bylaws and proprietary lease. Another thing that the Board and lady at the Private sector never mention about is the TIL. I found out about the TIL during the time I was in court with the Board last year (2013). The shareholders do not know anything about the TIL.

My advice to you is to check with the Authority on (address omitted). I sent about 50 pages of report to Authority, along with other documents (particularly court documents) and some recordings. Everything that I write about also included on the report with a lot of details. Making choices and decisions without knowing what is really going on the buildings (address omitted) can be very harmful, particularly to those who do not cause the problems. I also sent this letter on the behalf of the others who have been suffered from the same problems that we suffered. The board has been control by bunch of people who like to commit prejudice, discrimination, arrogance, ignorance, perjury, extortion, robbery, corruption, favoritism, and few more other problems such as illegal kicking out of the buildings. The board is also power hungry people because they think they can do whatever they want. I want you to know that this letter will send to the Justice Department, along with the copy of the bills that you send. Everything I sent to the Justice Department is based on my investigation, research, and report. I do not even get pay to do all of these works, but hoping that everything workout fine. I also sent letter to C*** I***** because they send a letter that was sitting on top of the mail boxes as returning mail this March 2014. I sent them letter explaining to them the reasons why the letter sent back to them as a returning mail.

Sincerely

Name omitted

Name omitted

Address omitted

Board information omitted for the purpose of the book.

• Sent to Authority

Part One: The outcome of Housing Court Part G: Case Index number (omitted). Date 6/16/14

(Holdover Proceeding)

On Friday May 30, 2014, I came from work in the morning and slept. My mother woke me up few hours later, told me that someone was downstairs at the lobby delivering paper to us. I went downstairs and got the paper delivered by someone who does not look like working for the Post Office. The paper delivered to us without envelop. I received the same paper on the next day (May 31, 2014) in the mail box along with 4 cards from the Civil Court. The same paper send on my father's name to pick up at the Post Office a day before court day (court date 6/4/14). I have to go to some problems to get the same paper on my father's absence. As I mentioned before that the Board (names omitted) know about my father's absence. When I came to court on the next day, the board lawyer was in the courtroom with his clients. He called me out few minutes before I saw the judge just to maintain his prejudice toward me as usual. He aggressively said to me that the landlord said that I must get out of the apartment. I told him that this is a CO-OP, and there is no landlord there. I find it so strange of the lawyer to ignore all the responses I sent to him since the HP-action cases up till April 2014. The lawyer is also under denial and pretentious about not receiving anything from me. I also find out that he happens to be the board personal lawyer. When the time came to see the judge, the judge wanted to close the case because there is no evidence to go on trial. Since the lawyer and his clients insisted to go on trial, they said yes. The judge asked me if I sent response to their lawyer. I said yes your honor. He said that to show it to him. I show it to him. The judge happened to take the first letter I sent to their lawyer and gave the rest. He asked me to sign in court and made a copy of it. The court kept the original and gave me the copy. The board and their lawyer did not give the paper that they sent to me three times to the court. I also let the judge knew that I received the paper that the board's lawyer had in his hand three times. The judge said the he needed everyone to come for the trial on 6/16/14.

Few days before the trial, I heard a meeting that would take place a day after court. I found about the meeting from one of the Haitians who told me about it. They received letter that was deliver under their door. I spoke with the one of the relatives who lives across the super about the meeting. He said yes he received the letter as well. The shareholder who knew about the unfair and illegal rent hikes told me that she received the letter and almost not receiving it. I told her that I was not invited at the meeting because I did not receive any letter. I spoke with the one of the shareholder who lives on the fourth floor one morning when I came from work about the meeting. He said that he did not know anything about the meeting. I told him that I was not invited at the meeting. I even sent email to **the Lady at the Private sector** about the not invited at the meeting. She never replied to my emails since I sent email to her about that I report all of the wrongdoing that has been going in the buildings.

I came back in courtroom 602 on June 16, 2014 and the Judge sent me and the board downstairs to room 501. I went to room 505 after nearly an hour and half later for the trial. When the time me to meet with the judge, the judge asked me question what right do I have to stay in my father's apartment. I said I have every right because it my father's apartment, we share the responsibilities, as well as the wife of the shareholder is there. The judge said things might come out differently on the trial which made me wondering what he meant by that. The president came on the stand and took summon. His lawyer asked him some questions and showed me papers. One of the questions had to do about that he is the president of HDFC and it is his business. He admitted that he lives in apt 3B. Their lawyer showed a document that happened to be the Proprietary Lease. I said to the judge that document could also be the Bylaws. I wave the one that the board gave me as the Bylaws before I went to court end of July of last year (2014). I was eager to contradict everything that they said. The Judge somehow stopped and told me that I would have my turn. It was already time for lunch. The Judge decided to hold on to everything and came at 2:30pm.

When everyone came back at 2:30pm, the president was still on the stand. When his lawyer did not have questions to ask him anymore, the judge asked me if I have questions for him. I asked him how he became president. His lawyer tried to mess that up, and the judge said overruled, this was a legitimate question. There was no answer given by the president. I asked him who is (CEO/Chair's name omitted). The judge kind of said to me that this question was wrong. I have plenty questions to asked, however I find out that they kind of questions I had unrelated to the case matter. When the judge asked me if I have other questions, I have no further questions. There was some shocking discovery I made during the time that the president was on stand. The lawyer who replaced the board's personal lawyer for the trial on HP-action (index omitted) was in the courtroom. I remembered he said that he replaced the board's personal lawyer. He never said anything about that he came from the same law firm with him. No wonder why the board's personal lawyer said that his law firm represented his clients all the way on the trial of the small claim. He sat in the back with the head when I turned my around. When I turned my head around again few minutes later, he was not in the courtroom. Keep that in mind the president said that we owed over $ 8,000 dollars on stand. I remembered he said that we owed $11,000 dollars in front of the shareholder who lives on the 4th floor in the building I lived, when he tried to spread lies and rumor while I was around the shareholder, outside of the buildings. The president said that we owed about $12000 dollars in court.

After the president took his stand, it was the head's time to stand and took summon. She admitted that she lived in apt 2B. Her lawyer asked her questions. One of the questions has to do about my father's absence. The same question was asking when the president was on the stand. They both were in denial to some degrees about my father's absence. When their lawyer got the list of the people's name for the apartments from the head, the lawyer showed it to me as well. It was the oldest lists of the people's name back in 1989. That list has been not been updated due to the reason that some of the shareholders move from one apartment to another and more. Some of the names were really faded on the list. I checked to see if my father's name spells right. I said to the Judge I had no comment. When the Judge asked her for the book that has the record of the rent payments, she said she left it home and forgot to come with it. When it was my turn to ask her question, I asked her if she really pay for her apartment. She was kind of angry when I asked her that question because I could see that on her face. She raised her eyes so wide and wanted to show a little anger. The Judge kind of said that question is unrelated. I said to the Judge I have no further questions. The head also said she has been in charge since 1989 when she took stand.

The Judge asked me it is my time to take stand and summoned. I was trying to go back to the bathroom floor situation, but the judge said to me that it was unrelated to the subject matter. All I did was to give him all the copies of documents I had ready for court. Most of what I give in court already sends to Authority. I send the rest of what I received from the board's lawyer for court. I also send other new documents. As I gave the judge documents, the board's lawyer asked to see the documents. He already knew about some of them, particularly about the HP action paper that printed out in court August 2013 which he knew about. One copy had been given to me; the other had been given to the president. He came to court alone, before he came to court with the others. The board's lawyer was against the notes I putted on the documents I gave to the Judge. The Judge said there is nothing wrong with that. I gave the judge the rest of the letters I sent to the board's lawyer and let the Judge knew that I came with the rest of the letter last time I was in court. The Judge collected them from me and putted with the one that the court collected from me on 6/4/14. I gave the judge all the copies of the 2013 payment receipts I made for my father. The board's lawyer asked to see them. The board's lawyer was under pretentious as usual about not receiving anything from me. He knew that I sent response to him, along with the copy of August and December 2013 receipt certified mail and regular mail. I said to the Judge that my father knew about the corruption, extortion, and robbery (monkey business exact words use in court) that happened in the buildings. I told the Judge that my father warned me about the buildings before he left, as well as knew what was going to happen in the buildings after the CEO/Chair, passed in 2008, the same year my father left. The illegal rent hikes that have been occurred in the buildings since her death up until now is one of the reasons. I told the judge that my father knew these problems had been going on for 33 years. I also let the Judge knew that my father said no one can take his name out of the apartment to replace him. I failed to let the Judge knew that my father knew about some people do not pay their fair share for three decades, as well as knew that some families are taking advantage over other families, particularly the people who are in charge of the buildings. I also failed to let the Judge knew about that my father keeps receiving mails, particularly mails about his medical information and bills. We either keep his mail for him or send them to Haiti. I did come with some of my father's mails in court, but forgot to show them to the Judge. I also let the Judge knew about the HP-action papers that the board's lawyer sent me, as well as showed the judge the copies of the envelopes. I let the Judge knew the envelopes sent to apartment 2B with my name on them. The Judge said that could be a mistake. I said it was not a mistake because the president signed the papers and said I live in 2B. I also let the Judge knew that I went to see the lady at the private sector twice during the time I was in court 2013. I let the Judge knew that she said some people do not pay nothing for 20 years, and they are taking advantage of my father. It happened to be the people who are in charge without mentioned anybody's name. The board's lawyer said he had no further questions. I let the Judge knew about when the board called police on me on 12/31/13. I already sent the copy of the letter to Authority on January 2014. What I wrote about what happened that day also repeated in court verbally. Everything that had been said in court on 6/16/14, also recorded. That was what the Judge said to me from the beginning about the reason why the microphones are around for in the courtroom. I also let the Judge knew that I sent all the papers I received from board's lawyers and sent them to Authority. I also let the Judge knew I would send all of the papers that I received from the board's lawyer for case # omitted, to Authority after court. I wanted the Judge knew that there should be investigation conducted on what has been going on the buildings, but failed to let the Judge knew about that. I even let the Judge knew that I had some recordings if he wanted to listen to them. The Judge said no, it was fine by shaking his head. I let the Judge knew that the Bylaws is fake because the same thing printing many times over.

The Judge that handled the trial happened to be the same judge I saw on the first HP action I filed against the buildings HP action index number: omitted. I kind of see the judge look familiar. I found out about that when he sent response to my father, as well as sent back all the papers I brought with me in court on (index number omitted). I send the copy of the letter the judge sends to my father's name to Authority. The Judge leaves everything the way the Board filed the "**John DOE and Jane DOE**" against me and my father. We are not the only one suffered from name misspelling on purpose. One of the shareholder's relative who live in the building I live (apt 2A) told me that no wonder why they keep their receipts safe. No wonder why father said to always make copies of the money orders after I write in them.

Part Two: The outcome of Housing Court Part G: Case Index number (omitted). Date 9/24/14

(Holdover proceeding case)

It was one Friday late at night around the hour of 6:30pm on September 2014 I received the Marshal notice. I found it shocking and surprised that the board went to the Marshal without the court order. The board never showed proof of anything in court, but only did things that would effectively back fire on them. the person who deliver the Marshal notice told me that it was the manager (name omitted) who order the eviction after I told him that I was in court with the board and they could never prove anything the board had against me in court. The person told me that it was the game that they are playing and I should go along with what they are doing. I went to the Marshal office which where the notice came from early in the morning on Monday. I have been told by the people who worked at the marshal's office that I must be in court right away the same day, and go to the second floor with the marshal notice. I went in court on the second with the notice and I happen to fill out a form given to me by the people who work on the second floor. The form indicates that what should I wrote and check that concerning about the issues and problems that have been occurred. I did all of that. The form was accurate to the response that I sent to the board's lawyers (**G*****& L*** PLLC**), and the court collected from me before and during the trial of the Holdover Proceedings. I have been told to go to see the Judge after the form has been collected from me. The Judge was surprised to see me come back to court as he stepped in the courtroom. When I approached the Judge, he told me that someone who would step out to talk to me about what should I do next. He also said that I have to go to serve the board's lawyers the same day so that the board and their lawyers had to be in court a day later (**on Wednesday**) because this could not wait. I did what have been told by the court. I found out that the board's lawyers were behind the eviction as well. The court did not know about it until the record print out and the board's lawyers happen to be the ones who ordered the eviction. I thought the board went along to the Marshal office to do the eviction without their lawyers' involvement.

I was surprised when I found out that the board and their lawyers did the same thing that they did on the HP action trial. The first lawyer who represented them for the Holdover trial did not show up. The other lawyer came to court instead. The board and their lawyers tried to change what they already have. That was the same thing they did during the HP action case. The judge said there was a trial and I lost while he wrote on paper. I responded how can I lose your Honor? I received your paper. The Judge replied, if you think you are not lost then make an appeal. When he gave me and the board's lawyer copies of what he wrote on. I was confused and shocked. What the Judge said verbally is totally different at what he wrote on the paper. I did not hear the part that he said to make an appeal because I was upset with the wrongdoings that the board and their lawyers had been doing in court. I heard the about making the appeal's part when I received the audio transcripts. I would not be able to go further explaining in details of what had been happened during the time of the eviction. I will let the letters that I sent to the Judge speak for themselves. I send the letters along with other documents. I want you to know that HPD is now; knowing what had been going on because I send court documents to the person who sent the bills on July 2014. I send documents twice to that person.

There are two things the Authority has to know. The first thing is that on the day of the trial the Board (names omitted) took pleasure about kicking me and my mother out of the apartment illegally. The Marshal and the police whom the Marshal called witness everything. On the day I came to get some of our belongings out of the apartment, the board left a trial of dog poop led from the bottom stairs to the front of our apartment. It seems to me that doing so is way to make it look like we are the one who did that. The poop was dried, and it was raining that day (Saturday of the same week that eviction took place). The second reason is that I have been blamed for not doing anything about the Judge decision. The lawyer that I hire after the eviction said it, as well as people who work in court said it. The lawyer who charged me $1700 dollars to take case robbed me, as well as giving wrong meaning of the Judge's decision. I asked him to give me my money when find out I have been bamboozled by him. He denied everything and blamed me by saying I was trying to vacate the Judge's decision. I send my case to the 3rd floor along with his response that he sent to me, to have cases against him at the end of March 2015. I knew and understand what the Judge decisions are because he wrote his decision based on what I have in my response. The lawyer that I hire to take care of the case told me that the Judge is wrong and the case should go to Supreme Court. He also charged for something that the court already knew about. He denied everything that he said and done. He did not even asking to see my exhibit. He was the one who called the Board's lawyer to set up an appointment to get our belongings out of the apartment. I send few other envelopes that had been send to me along with envelops that the board's lawyers send to me during the eviction.

Part 6

Appeal, what seems to be the problems?

The end of part five explained briefly about what I had to go through to have the appeal done. It was also sounded and seemed to be easy about making the appeal, when it was not. I thought I would go to the floor I should go to, in order to submit all of the paper works, paid the fees, and the court would do the rest. That was the opposite. I was the one who should do all of the work. I looked at the appeal as if nothing would ever solve if I did not make move at all. I was the one that should come to court, went on the floors I should went, to have the paper works done. The first step was to go to a place to have paper work notarized. The second step of the appeal was to serve the board's lawyer. I had to make trip the same day at the post office to send envelopes to the board lawyer(s) certify mails. I had to go back to court the same day to complete the rest of the appeal and made sure that there were no mistakes on what I sent to the board's lawyer(s). Otherwise, I had to start over if there were any mistakes. I had to do all of the paper work in one day without missing anything. Otherwise I had to come back in court on the next day to start the whole process again and paid fees again. There are more details and steps to go through while dealing with the process of the appeal at the NYC housing court websites. I just simplified things there about the steps.

I had to be in court early in the morning to make the appeal in case if the court crowed with people. It always takes time to have paper work done in the downtown court due to a lot of people coming in court to take care of their businesses. I had to live work in the morning, to spend my time in court to have the appeal done. It took me about six hours to have the appeal done. I had one day left since the illegal eviction took place to have the appeal done. I did not want to get blame by anyone in court saying that I had a month to do the appeal, and my time just passed. That was what the first court officer told me to some degree when legal aid office sent me to the floor to start the appeal, after legal aid found out they could not do anything about my case. I was under suspicion that the first court officer was trying to discourage me, to give up about the appeal. The first court officer told me that wait for the court officer who worked on the floor to come back from her break because she relieved her for break. The court officer told the other court officer that it was fine to do the appeal, after the court officer who relieved the other court officer for break explained about my situation.

It was the court officer who said indirectly about not to go spending money on lawyers in case like mine because I would lose the money, while taking care of the paper work for me. No wonder why I had to go back to the lawyer who stole my money and nearly jeopardized everything for me. The lawyer who stole my money was ambiguous about what he said to me over the court case. The lawyer told me that the Judge was wrong about everything. The lawyer also told me that the downtown court was a small court and the court case must go to the Supreme Court. That was evident that some lawyer had been committed wrongdoings in court and get away with them because it is a small court and have no respect for the court, particularly not having respect for the Judges (Female Judges). That was also evident that board and their lawyer(s) disregard what the Judge decision was on papers because they thought they could do whatever they wanted because they have no respect for the court. That also prove that a lot of people would always get hurt and vulnerable in the downtown court because the court is unable to protect them and they are on their own to deal with their problems. These people would end up left alone to figure out what to do on their situations. However, the lawyer switched his tone on me after he took my money. The lawyer told me that he could not represent me in court because he did not want to embarrass by the Judge said to him that it was useless for him to be in court when he knew what the Judge's decision means. Therefore, I found it shocked and surprised of the lawyer blaming me that I tried to vacate the Judge's decision.

I also found absurd of the lawyer blamed me not telling him about the Bylaws was faked. He was the one who asked me about the Bylaws in the first place. I found it strange of him to ask me about the Bylaws instead of the Proprietary Lease. The Judge did not mention anything about the Bylaws on his decision, but only about the Proprietary Lease. I wondered why the Judge did not include the Bylaws on his decision. The lawyer even asked me about the board's address to make the shitty and worthless appeal. I told him that the board did not have an address. The lawyer did not say anything. I was also under suspicion that the lawyer might blame for not showing the exhibits, since I came with everything in his office during the day he and his assistant did the shitty and worthless appeal. The lawyer did not even ask me if I had response on paper collected in court. He ended up read the Judge decisions and draw conclusion without looking at all of my exhibits and response. No wonder why the lawyer gave me the shitty and worthless appeal without his name and his law firm on the appeal because the lawyer wanted to stay anonymous on that. The lawyer also knew that the shitty and worthless appeal was not going to work.

I remembered almost in a month later, after I left the court after the trial of the hold over proceeding and went to the Supreme Court to file article 78 against a City Agency, after the City Agency tried to disqualify me of an exam I passed with high grade. The City Agency was partially clear and specific on paper about where to go to do the Article 78 in the Supreme Court. The City Agency failed to tell me where exactly I should go to in the Supreme Court, to start the Article 78. I had to ask where to go for that while I wandered in the Supreme Court (*I did not know the result of that case since it has been transferred to another place, after the Judge made his/her decision on paper. I received the Judge decision few days after I was evicted illegally. No one seems care to call me in case a letter or envelop sent back to them as returning mail*). I witnessed a client, who came to file case against the Private sector, which made me wondered what kind of case she had against the public sector. The court employee, who helped the client, asked her if she had a lawyer. The client responded yes, she had a lawyer. The employee told her that her lawyer must do all of the paper work for her since she paid her lawyer. No wondered why I had to build case against the lawyer not only on the robbery he committed, but also I was bamboozled and blamed by the lawyer. The lawyer also used me as his slave to do his work for him while charged me for the work. The lawyer also used me as scapegoat (patsy) to blame all of the problems that he caused to me as I mentioned before.

Two women I spoke to about my problems and issues worked in the law firm I used to work at night. The first woman, a secretary, told me that her lawyer charged her a lot of money of a case she helped her father solved. The first woman added that she done all of the paper work herself. She told me that all of her lawyer did was to represent her in court said few words that was it. She told me that it was an option to pay what a lawyer asked you to pay him/ her as fees. That was what she did. The first woman asked me if the lawyer who stole my money has been nasty to me. I responded yes. The first woman told me that I should have reported about the lawyer to the place where lawyers got their licenses, in order to have the lawyer's license revoked. I told her I already reported everything to the Justice Department. The first woman told me what the board and their lawyer(s) did to me was "identity theft". The woman added that it was great that I knew what I was doing by taking care of everything myself. The second woman, another secretary, told me that the board and their lawyer(s) served me and sent papers late to me; so that I would not have time to prepare and send back response to them. She was right about that.

There was a website that I found out about how long the appeal would take on October 2016. It took me while to get access to the website miraculously. The website stated that the appeal takes one year and a half to be solved. The appeal started few months after filling out for the appeal, on the day that everything sends to the Supreme Court. The website also stated that it depends on the cases because some cases might take more than one year and a half to solve. That proved that the situation in the buildings I lived in is far deeper than anyone could ever imagine. The person I chose from the list that the court had, to do the appeal was right about that the appeal could take longer to solve. The downtown court had to spend at least few months from the day I filed for the appeal and chose the person from the list that the court has in order to send the audio and written transcript to. I also received most of the audios of what had been recorded on the trial, and on the day that I was going to be evicted illegally. I did not receive the recording of what the first Judge said and what the Judge who held the case said on the day he was surprised that I came back in court; and found out that the board and their lawyer(s) went against his decision to evict me from the apartment. I was lucky enough to keep these records of what had been said in court in writing as my personal records. The person I chose from the list that the court had to take care of the appeal told me that she had to read about over hundred pages of written transcript on the first day I met with her on December 31, 2014. I did all the work myself, and I do hope that someone would come out of nowhere to rip the benefits of what I done without any help from anyone. I also do not hope that anyone overcharge me by saying that they did work which they have no prove of. I did all of the work just to make sure that it would take less time to have the appeal solve. However, that is how the system is and works because it does not matter if one person did all the work; it would take the minimum or maximum time the system set forth to have the appeal done. The appeal should have been solved within six months due to all the work I done. Therefore, I have done all of the investigation, research, and report all by myself. I also discovered that the housing situations, problems, and issues can be solved if every individual who suffer under the hands of the people in charge of their buildings, done the same type of work I did, even better than mine; to deal with their housing situations, problems, and issues effectively. Otherwise, putting faith on their lawyers to solve their housing situations, problems, and issues can be risky not only on spending on lawyers, but also the guarantee that the lawyers would take care of their housing situations, problems and issues appropriately, properly, and effectively. All I see some lawyers doing court is like to have repetitive clients because they want to charge their clients every time these lawyers represent their clients in court.

The lady I chose from the list that the court gave me, told me she had to spend a month to read the written transcript, and listen to the audio transcript, to prepare everything and send them to where she supposed to send them without given me information where. These few months were not included on the one-year and a half to have the appeal resolved, on the website I checked about the process to do the appeal. Therefore, it will take longer than I thought to have the appeal resolve while I suffered out there. The court and the lady did not even get in contact with me, to find out how my life was. I reached out to the Judge and the lady that I chose from the list to take care of the appeal. None of them seemed to care about how my life was. They knew for facts that I would suffered under this illegal eviction. The lady I chose from the list to take care of the appeal told me that there was a building near where she lived in downtown suffered from landlord's problems. I never thought that the landlord problems would be in area she lived in because the area inhabited by people who made a lot of money.

The other parts had to do about the appeal itself. There are three situation that that may appear as problems while dealing with the appeal. The first situation had to do about having another person to send envelopes to the other party who caused the eviction. The second situation has to do about that to have another address other than the address of which that the person was evicted from. The third situation has to do about not knowing how long the appeal would take to solve. These three situations would explain in details below. These three situations also found on the website I found information about the process for the appeal.

The first situation had to do about having another person to send envelopes to the other party. That person only happens to be the person to do that, other than the person who was in court with the other party. That person can be a stranger, friends, or family members. However, there can be problems among the three. How can I trust a stranger to serve the other party for me? I have to spend money for that. There is no fix fees and amount of money I have to pay a stranger to do the work for me. Therefore, the stranger can charge me any fees which base on choice and decision. How can there be any guarantee that the stranger would do the work for me base on ethics and agreements. The stranger might end up stealing my money and does not do the work. Therefore, I may get blame by the court that even though it was the court which designs the appeal to be done that way. In a case like mine, it was very crucial for me to put my hope and faith on strangers.

There are few problems that may happen when it comes to friends and family members. One of the few problems has to do about what if my friends and/or family members live far away from where I live, to help me with the appeal. What if I happen to be the only person live in New York City and all my friends and families living in other States; or other boroughs, Albany, and Long Island? The other few problems have to do about bothering my friends and families to help me with the appeal when they have their own business to deal with, such as work and personal businesses that they might deal with on a daily basis. The State of New York is a State that that people do not have time for anything, as well as people do not want to be bothered. Even those who never do anything, as well as have enough time, do not want to be bothered. Therefore, New York City happens to be a place where alienation, arrogance, irresponsible, carelessness, and ignorance is high to some extent because some people do not care, as long as they are not the one suffer from the problems that occur in the city.

Even the people who should have helped me, ended up not doing so, but transfer the problem to others and nothing work. That was what happened for almost three months after the illegal eviction took place. Therefore, I ended up fed up and discourage to keep going to places for help when I did not have time to do so. The last place I went to get help not only for me but also for all the problems that happened in the buildings. That place was the government local's office that located in (address omitted). That was the third time I went there and never went there anymore. The first time I went there as I mentioned before was during the HP action case. The second time was a week after the eviction took place. The third time was in November 2014. The person I went to see in his office gave me such confidence that he would take all of the paper work from me. He was the one who told me to come with all of the evidence on the next day after I told him that I had all of the evidence. However, everything completely changed when I came on the next day, along with the copies of the evidence. These evidences were the ones that I sent to Authority and collected in court during the trial of the holdover proceeding. The person read the second decision that the Judge wrote on the holdover proceeding case, and told me to forget about the first decision because the first decision that the Judge made was useless. The person ended up gave me two addresses of legal aid offices that he wrote on a sheet of paper, to go to do an appeal. He got rid of me in less than five minutes without collecting the copies of evidence I brought to him. I wasted my time making copies of all the evidence collected in court on the trial of the holdover proceeding. The person even gave me his card on the first day I met with him at his office. The way the person got rid of me was strange and weird. He called me to seat from one place to another, almost every ten seconds before he told me to go back from the entrance and waited for him. The person did not even know where to go to do the appeal. I told him that the appeal had been after he gave me the address of the two legal aid offices.

I had been in legal aid office before and the legal aid office ended unable to do anything about my case due to the complexities surrounding my case. The legal aid office I went to may be in some trouble after the people worked in there, made me wasted my time. Therefore, I had no choice, but only report to the Judge who held the trial of the holdover proceeding, since it was the court, which gave me the list of addresses of legal aid office to go to for my case. I also wondered if the people who work for the court, the ones I saw for my case, were prejudice and careless, otherwise they just lazy to do their jobs. It is easy to put addresses on papers, give them to somebody, instead of calling one place from the list, and tell them that I will come over for my court case. Even the list that the court gave me needed to be updated because one of the addresses was not there. The building had been bulldozed. That address was located not far away from the Housing Court. I also wonder why the legal aid I went to, did not help me finding a place to live since they know that I was evicted illegally. What is the purpose of legal aid offices? Do they here to help tenants finding places to live in time of problem regardless the type of buildings that the tenants live?

After everything that I had been through, no wonder I why I did all of the work myself in all of the court cases, in order to prevent to go to other people for help, when they could not help me. It was the court, which should take all of the blames of what I had been through on the appeal issue and problem. It was the court, which allows me to go through all of the problems; I faced during the illegal eviction. The court could have done all the work themselves about the appeal. A little bother of person whom I though was my best friend had been in housing court in downtown Brooklyn, found out the court is a strange, weird, and ridiculous place to be. He was the one who told me that, it was the court, which should pay the fees to do the appeal and I did not have to do anything. We met miraculously the second time early November 2016, and met the first time in the middle of October 2016. We met across the street of the Buildings while we were in our ways, taking care of our business. I showed him some of the evidence that I had about the buildings. He was surprised that I took all of the responsibility of the buildings myself without any help. He also surprised how I got money to pay for everything, as well as the time and energy to do all of these work. I had to make the time to deal with the buildings problems because I had to no choice. The board and their lawyers ended up creating problems for me and my parents, which could not be ignored. The board and their lawyers also created problems for the buildings, themselves, and everybody else, which also could not be ignored. I do care about what happened in buildings, as well as what is at stake for us and for the buildings.

The second situation has to do about that to have another address other than the address of which that the person was evicted from. In other words, I cannot use the address I was evicted from to do the appeal. I must do the appeal to a different address. I find this part weird and problematic for some reasons. I did not have anywhere to go on the day that I was forced out of the apartment illegally by the board and their lawyers, the marshal, and the police. My mother and I had to go to her friend's apartment the same day, which was a big, surprised for them. My mother and I were lucky that her friend and her daughter took us in, and provided us with private shelter, not rent. I had to use their address to make the appeal even though they did not want us to use their address to do anything on. I had to pay fees to them three months later (January 2015) due to the reason that the appeal may take longer to resolve. I thought that the appeal would go through and resolve quickly. Spending more than three months without a home is more than enough pain, problem, and suffering to bear emotionally, spiritually, and mentally. The illegal eviction served to me as if I was some kind of criminal, which serving time outside of the apartment; unable and uncertain to know how long my sentence would be over or last.

My mother and I effectively brought our problems to her friend because I did not want the landlord used us as an excuse and advantage to get my mother's friend out of the apartment. Otherwise, there is no problem at all. I could help them if it comes to that. However, they would not need me to help them because that is their apartment. They would unable to fight for themselves if they did not seek my help on that. I also could not leave the apartment for two reasons. The first reason had to do about the appeal. I did not know if the appeal would get affected if I leave the apartment. The second reason has to do about my mother. She does not want to be far away from her church, as well as everything she does in her personal life. She had been living in the neighborhood since end of 1996, and got used to it. Relocated her could be a problem for her. She would unable to adapt herself to different environment. The illegal eviction affected her so deeply. She is one of the main the reasons I try to get the apartment back.

Otherwise, I would go to a shelter if it was not for her, dealing with all of the nonsense and stupidity.

There was another countryman of mine who used to work for a client in the building I used to work at night, suffered from getting an apartment in the city. He told me that it is hard for him to rent one decent room from anyone. He told that someone tried to rent him one room that is dirty for more than six hundred dollars a month. He just bailed out and remained where he was. My condition was worse than his condition. My mother and I had four feet wide and six feet long of space available in the room, which not a bedroom, along with a lot of belongings which were not ours. I ended up paid a lot of money for that small space (from $400 to $575 per month for both of us). I would like to do something about the room but unable to do so because my mother's friend and her daughter would not allow it. There were few problems in the room, which I would not say anything about them. The same countryman told me that she tried to get her mother to come to New York but unable to do so because he did not have a place to live with his mother. He told that his mother values her privacy a lot and unable to live and share space with anyone else. Therefore, his mother had something in common with my mother there. I have to spend most of my time out on a daily basis and pretend that my life has been nothing but a dream. Doing so is a way not to let problem affected me so deeply which may lead to the rise of my blood pressure. My blood pressure had been high and gotten higher during the last two months I was evicted. I would, should, or could have been in trouble if I went to see doctors. I may end up taken prescriptions for the rest of my life. Blood did not circulate on certain part of my body for two months straight. It was not until beginning of December 2014 I started to get better. It was only one person took deep look of me, and felt the energy or vibes on me during that two months. She worked in the law firm I used to work at night. She told me one night that I looked deeply hurt of something that happened to me. I told her that I was evicted illegally in my apartment.

I also find it so strange that the court system designs to do the appeal that way because how in the hell I would find a place right on the spot to do the appeal, after I was evicted illegally. The court knew effectively that the City suffered from housing problem that resulted to a lot of people dislocated, and gentrification is the result to that. Therefore, it is absurd of the court to design an appeal this way. Otherwise, the court wanted me to remain evicted because the court knew that the case I had against the buildings was enormous. The court found out that the price that would pay to me is bigger and no one seemed to pay the price for what happened to me. I am under suspicion that I would not get anything based on the way things had been going on with the appeal.

I ended up send letters to the Judge about a lot of issues and problems; particularly about living in the address I used to do the appeal. I let the Judge knew that the court would be held responsible and accountable if my mother's friend and her daughter happened to be in problem because we seemed to be in their apartment illegally. I found it absurd of the court to evict me and tried to find another address to do the appeal when it was impossible to find right away. The court also gives one month to start the process of the appeal, which also impossible to do without finding another address to do it right away.

The third situation has to do about not knowing how long the appeal would take to resolve. In other words, it is uncertain to know how long the appeal would be resolved. I also found it absurd of the court to make decision about evicted me; not knowing how long it would take to have the appeal resolved. The court should take responsibility to find a place for me to live if the court is uncertain about how long the appeal would take to resolve. The court should take responsibility about having someone else living in the apartment under our names on sub-letting. I could have stay in the apartment to do the appeal since the court found out that the board and their lawyers went against the Judge decision. Trying to find another address to do the appeal is dumb and stupid. The court must change that process on the appeal because it serves as trap for two reasons. The first reason is that the person may never find another address to do the appeal. Therefore, the person would take all the blame for not finding another address to do the appeal. The second reason has to do about that the court does not want the person to go through with the appeal for any reasons that I do not know about. I may speculate there to some degree. Let's go back to the second decision that the Judge wrote on paper. The judge told me to appeal his decision verbally, that I did not remember about it, as well as not written it on the paper. The Judge could have added on the paper that he made the second decision, along where to go to do the appeal.

The only thing that is useful about the appeal was to prove all of the wrongdoings that I faced in court by the board and board's lawyer(s). The book of Henry David Thoreau, on the duty of civil disobedience, explained the importance of the appeal. Having appeal done against someone was way to prove all of the wrongdoings that person committed against the victim.

I would never go through a lot, which I ended up robbed by a lawyer. Otherwise, the court used me as bait because the court wanted me to go through a lot to find out about lawyers that had been doing dirty work outside of the court. Therefore, the court must take responsibility to the fake and shitty appeal I got from the lawyer who robbed me. The court must take responsibility for not providing safety and security to us because the illegal eviction caused serious financial and social problem for us, particularly for me. I would never be able to get my mails since the apartment rented under our names on sub-letting. I was lucky enough to get a P.O. Box as soon as found out that I was unable to open the mailbox. However, it is not everything I can do on the P.O. Box because there are some mails I need to receive which require a house or an apartment to receive them. The law stated that a person must have a physical address to take care of his/her business. I knew about that on November 2016, when I offered to apply for credit card at Sear, to get higher percentage off the item I bought. The gentleman on the phone told me about the law, after I told him that I used the P.O. Box to get all of my mails. Otherwise, the envelope would send back to the company as returning mail if the company sends it to my address. I could not receive my bank statement from the address anymore due to those changes. I used to have all of my mails forwarding to the P.O. Box few months after I rent the P.O. Box, by using the building's address. However, the opportunity stopped all of the sudden. I have been told a year later that I have six months to have all of my mail to go the P.O. Box.

Another problem that the illegal eviction caused to me was about all of the Jobs that I apply for on the building's address, not the P.O. Box. Therefore all of the mails I may receive from these companies would send back to them if these companies happen to send me mails concerning about the positions that applied for. Most of these companies that applied jobs from are on the internet. I would not be able to change information about my address once I sent these applications electronically. I applied for a job on January 2015 and unable to go to take the exam for it in March 2015 because I was unable to open the mailbox, after I found out that the board rented the apartment. It was already too late when I received the mail, along with other mails. The shareholder was affected by the July 2010 fire, met with me one day miraculously, told me about that the shareholder below me pick up some mails for us which were left on top of the mailboxes. I was a week late to take the exam when I opened the letter. I kept using my credit card by using my mother's friend's address because of items I ordered online and unable to receive them on my P.O. Box.

The information that I found from the website which concerned about the holdover proceeding few months after the illegal eviction took place; only talked about the issues and problems surrounding buildings controls by landlords, not Co-Ops. Otherwise, it never makes any difference to some degree because the Co-Op boards may have the same mentality like the landlords. The Co-Op board of the buildings I live in behave the same way some landlords behave in court and outside of court, as well as mentally. The Co-Op board committed prejudice, discrimination, lying, and deceiving the same way some landlords would have committed them. The information on the website stated that a landlord can go against the Judge's decision to evict a tenant; when the landlord does not have proof why the tenant must be evicted. The tenant must leave the apartment without having argument with the Marshal because the Marshal is the employee of the court. The landlord must come back in court to bring evidence about the tenant's eviction; otherwise the landlord would be in trouble.

However, the website failed to provide enough information about the deadlines provided to the landlord to come to court, whether or not the landlord does not show in court, or else the court would intervene immediately. Therefore, the landlord may remove the Marshal Eviction paper from the door and rent the apartment illegally. That was what the board in the buildings did with my father's apartment. The board ended up renting my father's apartment under our names on sub-letting, by removed the Marshal's eviction paper on the apartment's door. I do not know how the tenant knew about the apartment. It was when I came to get my mails one Sunday afternoon in March 2015 and unable to open the mailbox. I had to ask him how did he know about the apartment and the apartment is on holdover proceeding. He told me that his lawyer found the apartment for him, which made me wonder which lawyer. Was it the board's lawyer, the lawyer who robbed me, or the lawyer whom my oldest sister and I went to see after I was robbed by the first lawyer? These were the only lawyers who knew about my case. Otherwise, there may be people who worked in court doing some kind of illegal activity anonymously just to make some quick bucks and leave mess behind. The movie, 99 homes (2016), was an example of that. The movie also showed examples of what I went through. The movie also show how corruption and falsify information and documents happened in court in order to steal properties illegally. There was another movie, wild cards (2015), also showed example of how trial handled in court to some degree. These two movies reminded me of what I went through in court.

After everything I have been through in court, I see the court as a place of duel where the defendants and the petitioners are the players or duelists, and the Judges serve as the referees and juries to some degree. The author of the book "Law and Society", Kitty Calavita, gives more details throughout her book about the way the court system works. I was glad that I read her book, which provided me with enough information about the way the court system is. I also use all of my abilities and capabilities to do the rest of the work myself. I was also lucky enough to learn about some theories and works on the field of Political Science, Sociology, Anthropology, Economics, and Liberal Arts. These fields also enable me to go on and use other works out there, in the environment I live to have some practical use of them. These fields also provide me both national and international education about the world. These fields also provided me the basic needs and help, to survive in life politically, socially, and economically. There is another book I began to read on April 2017. That book was very popular and caused controversial when it came out, and continued to be controversial. The book wrote by Howard Zinn, A People's History of the United States 1492-Present. Chapter three and chapter four of that book captured my attention. I saw that housing situation will always remain a problem in the country, particularly in New York City. I also see the reason why some people still do not have respect for the court and the Judge because they want things to go their ways regardless how mess up, backward, and wrong they are. No wondered I said that past, present, and future happen to have triangular reaction. I said that because the same problems of the past are still remained, but different strategies and tactics will always be used to get to the same things over and over again in the present and future. That is the vicious cycle. There was another that also captured my attention. The book wrote by John Holt, Freedom and Beyond. I discovered that book among of the books that were going to throw out as garbage. I chose that book among the others because its title captured my attention. I discovered that book during the time was in court with the board on the second HP action cases. I discovered that book in one of the site when I started to work for the employer in two months. I used to work overnight on that site twice a week. There was one thing among the others that capture my attention from the book. I will use that as an example of the buildings that I lived in. the buildings had been built since early 1930's and yet the buildings had been paid it dues many times over, even though some people may have had lived in them, did not pay anything. It is absurd to pay thousands of dollars in rent in a place that had been around for nearly a century. What kind of value is there in such place? It does not matter if the place is new or old; the money you pay for rent seems to never go down or remains constant. Otherwise, it is the greed of some individuals which make the place getting expensive and unaffordable, as well as they become freeloaders that never pay their fair share.

There is another book written by Raymond Fisman and Edward Miguel, Economic Gangsters. This book also captured my attention. It is quite evident that some people do behave like economic gangsters, particularly in illegal ways. Economic gangsters happen to be a global problem. That was what the board had been doing because they acted like economic gangsters and mafia. They think they can do whatever they want and get away with them. They ended proclaimed themselves as collectors and controllers of the buildings. They ended up being cowards when they came to court and sent me papers illegally and claimed that they were not in charge. There is another book written by David L.L. Shields, The Color of Hunger. I read this book about a decade ago. Some of what Howard Zinn talked in his book, found in that book. Above all, I watched a documentary about by the title IOUSA, which concern about the United-States national financial debt. The people who talked in the documentary worked for the government, and they showed evidence of what contributed to the national financial debt. I would like to know if the housing situation (including apartment buildings) contributed to the national debt as well. A special thanks to someone who had been helpful to me about the book. He advised about the book, as well as helps me to publish. I was lucky to have someone like this helping me even though he does not have time.

Someone I met in a building that I went to work for the first, on Martin Luther King's birth 2017 told me that the court is now discourage people from suing. I do not know if that is true. The court must stop the people who control the buildings (Co-Ops, Landlords, and Agencies) committed prejudice, discrimination, and injustice against the tenants, particularly when the tenants are innocent of wrongdoings. My cases have been used as examples.

Some people who are in charge do things on purpose that leads to carelessness, arrogant, ignorant, irresponsible and low self-esteem. They do bad things to the tenants, as long as they will not be the one to suffer the consequences of their actions. I learned about that from someone recently at work. A co-worker just got hired and few months later said in front of me and someone else that he does not care what he does to someone, as long as he was not the one to suffer the consequences of his wrongdoings. That was very careless, arrogant, ignorant, irresponsible, heartless, and low self-esteem of him. He thought he can do that to me, but ended up victimized by his owned wrongdoings. He ended up fired after he tried to do things to jeopardize my position at work. He thought he was smart regardless his class and race, as well as heard that he had people. He thought that anyone can put up with him even though the supervisor, the account manager, and the company never did anything when he committed offenses every day in six to seven months of his employment. He did more mess and major offenses than any one that could get fire over stupid things. He and the supervisor (including the one that replaced the supervisor) was the same people, even though the supervisor complained about him, but may seem to never write him up about his wrongdoings. I showed him that I was the last person he can ever mess with. Therefore, people like him would always remain in life. People like him are very sneaky, slicky, and sleazy. People like him put themselves in trouble and found somebody to go down with them, particularly by creating lies and rumors. People like him hated when they cannot get to somebody they cannot mess with. People like him make mess and want somebody to take responsibility of their mess. People like that remind me of the people (the board) in my buildings every time I have to deal with them. I decide not to include everything that I have been with the current and previous employers in the book. I have been through a lot during the time I have been evicted. There is one thing I want to say is that, it is better to work in a company that has Union. The Union will be able to help someone if that person able to save himself/ herself from his/ her employer prejudice and injustice; or if the prejudice and done by people who work for the employer. The case I had against my current employer is that turned out to be the second bigger case that I should have sent to the Justice Department. I did not do so because the Union got involved despite the fact that I continued to face prejudice and injustice toward those who caused the problem for nearly seven months. I sent the case I had against my previous employer to the Justice Department because of the prejudice and injustice I faced toward them. The reason why my previous employer had problem with me is that management, particularly the new account manager of the site I worked, did not take care of lies that the co-worker I used to work with at night, imposed on me. They ended up being on the co-worker side, as well as it was their mess of what happened that night. The reason I sent my case to the Justice Department is that there was no Union in the company to help me with my case. I ended up become expendable out of everything that happened to me.

Before I concluded the book, I have to go back from the first HP action one more time because it was important, as well as the crucial move I had to make. The Judge who held the trial of the Holdover Proceeding told me on the first HP action case that he cannot tell me what to do, I should figure it out, when I asked him what he wanted me to do after the board and their lawyer lied and accused me unfairly about I wanted to sue them, as well as I was not the shareholder. The Judge said what he said to me loudly for everyone to hear in the courtroom. I am under suspicion that the Judge was not only send message or signal to me, but to everyone who was in the courtroom that day. Therefore, everyone or every tenant has to fight his or her own fight. Despite all of the laws that set forth by the Government of the City of New York on housing, majority of the tenants would always ended up unprotected by these laws. I considered the issues and problems of housing just like tobacco, drug, money laundering, gun control, fast food, healthcare, and oil. All of these matters have economics reasons behind them. There is one more thing I need to say. I did the best I can to make sure that my father did not get affected by what had been going on during his absence. It will not be my problem if he loses the apartment. The judge did what he could to have the apartment under my father's name. It was the board and their lawyer(s) who messed that up when they went against his decision. What the board and their lawyer(s) did is to affect the well-being of my family, particularly mine since I happened to be the one dealing with their wickedness, pain, and suffering. I have been blamed by my family over everything. It could have been worst for us if I did not do anything at all. That is one of the main reasons that I publish this book, to show to the readers or audiences what I had been through all by myself. The end of the book has the letters or reports I sent to the Judge, along with the case I have against the lawyer who robbed me. These letters and documents also sent to Authority.

• Sent to Authority

Court case index: omitted

11/3/14

Note: name and address omitted for the purpose of the book.

Letter to Judge (name omitted for the purpose of the book)

Dear Your Honor

I send you this letter along with other documents to add in court file, to further the court case. I also want you to know that I file an appeal on the seventh floor, last week (10/29/14) to reopen both cases, particularly the first case that took place in June 2014. I want to do so because I have been blamed for not to do anything about the response that you sent to everyone. I heard that I had sixty to ninety days to do something about the response that you sent to everyone. I also heard that it is too late to do something about the problem due the reason that City Marshal took possession of the apartment. I did not know if I had to do something about it because I did not have a lawyer. I also did not know if I had to do anything about it since you sent response under my father's name and left it just like the board (**names omitted for the purpose of the book**) and their lawyer (**G***** & L***) did it (**Misspelling my father's first name on purpose**). At the same time, my father and I had been represented improperly. I want you to know that the wife of the shareholder, (name omitted), has been affected by what the board had been doing last year until now. ` She has been living in the apartment for more than fourteen years. I could not bring her to court since the board did not go after her. The board also did not want to deal with the response that you sent to everyone, particularly the fake president, who left his apartment for almost two months for not dealing with the response that you sent to everyone. He came back the same week he and the others served me with the Marshal Notice. No wonder he had an evil smile in his face when he saw me came in on Monday September 15, 2014, in the morning, after I left the Supreme Court that Monday morning. I was wondering what he was up to. The president and the super were standing outside of building I live, talking to each other. Another thing to know about the board and the super is that, particularly the president, they like to create lies to get people in trouble. We are not the only one who had been victimized by their lies. I sent you the copies of the papers that **G***** and L***** sent to me to see all of the lies and false allegations against me.

The fifteenth floor sent me to (**address omitted**) to see if they could do something about the problem. The person who took the case, known by the name (**name omitted**), told my mother and I that it was going to be very difficult to do something about the problem, as well as had limited of power to get access to the court file. He took a look at the Bylaws that the Board gave me last year and found out that the Bylaws was faked. He took a looked at Proprietary Lease that I brought in court on June 2014 and found. He also took a looked at the responses that I sent to the board's lawyer (**G***** & L***), that the court already had as record out that it was meaningless. He took a looked at the TIL and found out that the TIL is meaningful. I called him on Monday October 27, 2014, a week after he reviewed all of the documents I brought in court on June 2014. I was lucky I called him because he told me that there was nothing he could do about the problem because the problem was complex. He was the one who told me to go the seventh floor in the court just to see I could make an appeal. I also called the City Marshal office the same day, and found out that the board evicted us due the reason that the board does not want money from us.

I send you the rest of the documents because I sent them to Authority. There were things that the board said on audio which I could prove that they are faked. You may choose to send them back to me when you done with them. I have a lot of copies of them electronically and hard copies. I also want to fix two things I put on writing and said in court. The first thing I want to fix about when I said the lady at the Private sector knew about my father's absent. She did not know about my father's absence until I sent email to her, explaining the reasons why my father has been absent. I told her that the board knew about my father's absence, particularly the head. My father told her that my mother and I would take over the apartment, before my father left in 2008, few months after the death the CEO/Chair. The board never told the lady at the Private sector about my father's absence. She already told me I could exit in for my father which I do not know how this could accomplish. I also put on my response that the Public sector knew about that I live in the apartment. I meant to say a branch from the Public sector. I sent information about my mother and I last year (2013) twice. I let them knew about that we were against the rent hikes last year (2013) as well as sent some of my report about what has been going in the buildings. The person who was handled the work told me over the phone that her job is on the line due to the reason that the board reported that the CO-OP is for senior citizens. The person also sent No wonder why the board did not want me to include my name on the branch for the Public sector application after the board raise the rent last year and claimed verbally that the shareholders make the decision to raise the rent, particularly in 2009 or 2010. The situation about raising the rent last year 2013 was worst. The board tried to raise the rent on some shareholders, particularly to all the Haitians. One the shareholders who got the paper about the rent hikes 2013, went in the buildings that I live in, to talk to the shareholder who live below me about the rent hikes. The shareholder, who lives below me, told her that he did not know any papers about the rent hikes. The shareholder next door (from the other building) called someone at the Public sector and called the lady at Private sector. They both told her that they did not know anything about the rent hikes. The rent hikes 2013 occurred by the board and their families, on a meeting that took place on March or April 2013. The meeting about the rent Hikes had been postponed many time before it was actually taking place. The meeting turned into disaster just like any other meetings held by the board in the past. The shareholder, who discovered about the illegal rent hikes, was the meeting and told me that the lady at the Private sector decided to raise the rent on everyone, since was not in the meeting. I sent you the copies of the rent hikes to you your Honor. No wonder why the board could not come with the book that handles the rent record in court June 2014. However the lady at the Private sector would always take the side of the board, as an assistant who failed to do her job. Some shareholders are under suspicion that she might take money from the board to keep her mouth shut about all the wrongdoings that the board committed. She knew for facts that the board does everything wrong.

Another thing I want to be clear when I came to court on September 22, 2014, about the bills of the buildings are due. I said that the buildings owed almost $500,000 dollars. The number is less than that. The buildings owe nearly $300,000 dollars. I sent response to the person who sent bill at Public sector. I talked to that person over the phone last year 2013. He was the one who told that the board is responsible for the physical structure of the apartment during the time I was court with the board on the HP action case, after I brought the board on trial. The person also told me that he knew about the buildings for a very long time. However, he did not know if the board lives in the buildings. I even went to see the person during the same week I was evicted in the apartment. The board seemed to tell the Public sector that we owed on monthly rents that is why they kick us out. I showed the person all of the money orders I make for my father for the rent. I sent all documents that I brought in court on June 2014, as well as everything that I send to you your Honor to that person. I want to open the case for another reason is that I have been told by some shareholders that the board wants to sell my father's apartment. No wonder why I asked them to bring records of the Stock Certificates for everyone, including themselves. If we happen to get out of the apartment, they board would do just like they did to the apartment next to us (apt 2C). The board kicks the child of the shareholder's out during the year 2010 and rent the apartment that is not registered under the name of the people who live in it. There are five apartments in both buildings that are like that, as well as five apartments may register under the name of the people who live in them, which are not shareholder. I knew the situation about the apartment 2C from the cousin of one of the board who lives on the third floor. I knew something was wrong with the apartment when I did research on every apartment in both buildings before he told me about the problem later on the same day that the board called police on me on January 3, 2014. He told me that the board is doing the same thing to me, as well as trying to screw me on the rent payment. Maybe **G***** and L***** had to do about the all of these illegal kicking out since I found out that the board hired them as their primary lawyers. Apartment 2C may still register under the name of the shareholder who used to live in them. I tried to remember what the President said about there are about sixteen apartment or less opened in both buildings on the audio. I send you the information that you need to contradict what he said in court June 2014. The board even tries to kick some shareholders out, particularly the Haitians. No wonder why some shareholders were under suspicion about that one of the board relatives may set fire on the roof of the building of (the other building) on 4th of July 2010 going to be 5th of July 2010 in the morning. The board effectively knew who set the fire on the roof of the other building since they have set up cameras around for more than four years, even before the fire occurred. Most of what I have on papers here your Honor, are the summary of what I have on my report that I sent to Authority. I am under Oath on them.

Sincerely

My name omitted

Address omitted for the purpose of the book.

From (Name omitted)

Court case index: omitted

From 3/10/15 to 3/12/15

Judge (name omitted)

Address omitted for the purpose of the book

Letter to Judge (name omitted for the purpose of the book)

Dear Your Honor

I send this letter in the response of the letter that sent by you from the lawyer who represents you. I want you to know that I have no intention to include anyone in the case. I just let them knew what is going because the buildings are supposed to be under their watch, particularly the lady at **the Private sector**. She is kind of accessory to everything that happened to me, as well as what has been going in the buildings. She knows about all the wrong doing that the board did. No wonder why some of the shareholders are under suspicion about her taking bribe to keep her mouth shut about all the wrongdoings done by the Board (**names omitted**). She also knew about that I have been in court with the board (from the HP action to the Holdover Proceeding). She also knew about the fake Bylaws, as well sent her the response about what the board's lawyers (**G***** and L*****) sent to me during the HP action cases. She personally told me that not to send response to the lawyer because lawyers do not read after she discovered that I can cause serious problem to her and the Board based on what has been going on. She also told me that the Judge was wrong when I let her knew that the first judge from the second HP action told me I must sent response to the board's lawyer based on what he would sent to me. She even threatens that I have been sued without showing ground, causes, and evidence of that. She was also contributed at hire lawyers (**G***** and L*****). All of this conversation took place at her office; behind closed doors, as well as I have some of them by emails. She did not really welcome me well at her office, the second time I came to see her. She also stopped respond from my emails after the board called police for me. She was also contributed into kicking me out of the apartment. There was a meeting that took place a week before thanksgiving in 2013 and she said loudly in front of the few shareholders and the board about to kick me out and charged lawyer's fees under my father's name. As

I said before only few shareholders were invited, the others did not invite. I have been forced by her and the board about to keep my mouth shut in the meeting if I do fill out some illegal paper that could use against me in the future under my father's name to attend at the meeting. That meeting was also had to do about the trial of the HP action 2013. That meeting was used as a way to threat me, as well as brought fear to me. As for person from **the Public sector**, he also knew about the buildings along time. It was him that I spoke over the phone in October 2013 about the HP action case. It was him who told me that the physical structure of the apartment is the board responsibility. That had been used against the board during the trial of the HP action case December 2013. He also told me over the phone that the board would never let me become shareholder if I brought them in court. It was him that I sent response to after I received the bills of the buildings, along with few other documents which the court collected from me on the trial of the Holdover Proceeding 2014. It was him that I saw during first week after the eviction date started. He had told me that the board kicked me out because I did not pay the rent. I showed him proof that I paid the rent and the rent had been refused by the board. He also thought that I went in court unprepared, as well as had the assumption about that come to court unprepared. He even said that the Judge would rule over me even though I was right about everything because I do not have a lawyer to represent me. Therefore, I decided to send him all the court papers for the holdover proceeding, as well as the papers that the board's lawyers sent to me on the HP action cases and the response that I sent to the Board's lawyers. I sent the response that you sent and the response that the court collected from me before the trial of the Holdover Proceeding case, just to show him that he wrong and never judges a book by its cover. The board, particularly the president stated and signed that he had sent the HP action papers that their lawyers sent to me to **the Public sector**. These HP action papers sent to you your Honor, in November 2014, to add them to the court file. Therefore, the person at the Public sector and the lady at the Private sector knew about all the wrong doings that the board done. They did not do anything at all.

I also want to know what the court will do about the illegal rent that is going in my father's apartment right now. I want to know if the court really gives the board possession of the apartment, or the Marshal has been taking bribe by the board to open the apartment for rent, or the board took liberty at removing the marshal notice from the door and rent the apartment under my father's name. **I want you to know that I am not making any accusation here, but just trying to find out which one of what I wrote above going on here.** I also find it unfair and unacceptable to be homeless with my mother (63 years old) for almost six months. It seems to me that nobody gives a damn about that. We have been doing our fair share without missing out on the rent, and the people who do not pay anything for over 20 years, as well as those who miss out on the rent, still living large as if they own the buildings, particularly the board and board's families, since the board and their families tried to raise the rent on few shareholders early 2013, particularly on all Haitians in the buildings **(that was what the lady at the Private sector told me on the first meeting with her. She also adds that some shareholders are taking advantage of my father and some of them happened to be the board).** One of the shareholders found out about it and the meeting that had been postponed many times, eventually went into disaster when it finally happened. The board's meetings always go in disaster. The one that took place in July 2014 also went in disaster because it was also had to do about the Holdover Proceeding case. That shareholder happened to be the one that the board, particularly Mr. President tried to kick her out while her apartment affected by the fire that took place in July 2010. She was homeless as well for probably six months or more.

The board was surprised about that I use the **TIL** against them in court. The other shareholders did not know about the TIL. I gave few of them the TIL and hope they knew how to use it. The lady at the Private sector never said anything about the **TIL** as well, when I actually found the TIL at the **Private sector's** website in November 2013 during the HP action case going on. I should have used the TIL against the board on the HP action trial, but I did not because of the way the trial went. Therefore, the lady at the **Private sector** told the board to raise the rent on everyone. I find it as a failure of the court and the government, particularly local government, for not really doing anything at all. The account of the buildings should have been frozen already after what has been going on to us. The board finds ways to still collect the rent while they are in hidings. One more thing, the Marshal even called police on me when I explained to him as well as showed him that the board had been used faked names to evict us. He did not give a damn about that. I did the same thing to the police, and they did not give a damn about that as well. I also sent letter to the precinct after the board called police on me the second time in January 2014. I explained briefly on the paper that the police were helping the people who caused the problems, except the police who came in December 31, 2013. I even went to file complaint on the cops who showed up in January 3, 2014, as well as on the board at the precinct. They did not do anything. They just ignored me, as well as being careless. I even check local government, especially the people that I voted for. They did not do anything as well. No wonder why I sent over fifty pages of report to the Justice Department about what has been going on in court and outside of the court. I hope the Justice Department does something about not only the problems, but also about the **financial crimes** and **illegal gentrification** that are going on in the buildings. The board probably used the buildings finance for their private gain. It is also evident that the board use false names to evict us. The Lady from HPD SCRIE happened to be the first one whom I sent courts documents to (HP actions) and the complaint about what has been going. She sent them back to me along with a letter. The letter also indicated that I should send my issues and complains to 311 which I did in January 2014. 311 did not do anything about the problem. I tried department of buildings after one of the police officers told me to approach him after the President called police on me due to the illegal fees he charged my father for December 31, 2013. I have that recorded as well. I want you to know your Honor that the lady at the **Private sector** listened to the first recording I made, the one that I included on the bathroom floor incident I wrote. She listened to it while I paid her visit for the first in her office, after I left court on the first HP action. I also find that ironic that she still listens to the board, particularly the president, after they lied to her about everything. I explained to the police officers about the reasons for calling the police on December 31, 2013. One of them told me to call department of Buildings. He told me that 311 would never do anything. I called department of Buildings in January 2014, and had been told that they do not take care of CO-OP business and directed me back to 311. The Lady at the branch of the Public sector told me that her job is on the line based on what the board sent to her, was different to what I sent to her, particularly about the misspelling of my father's name on purpose. She also told me that the CO-OP is an elderly CO-OP when I talked to her over the phone. Therefore, the board has been lying not in court, but also outside court.

As I said before, does the court do anything about this illegal rent that has been going on in my father's apartment? I also want to know if the court does something about the problem already. It is also making the court looks so bad because it is unable to keep tackle the problem. As I stated on the report that I sent to Authority, that I did most of the work for them without getting pay for it. They should do the rest. The same thing goes to the court as well. I also hope to hear from the court about the illegal rent that happened in my father's apartment. As I said before, your honor, everything that I have on the paper is available on the report with a lot of details about them.

Note: I want to know who fixed the apartment. Is it the court or the board? If it is the board, the board has to show where the money is coming from since the buildings owed hundreds of thousands of dollars. The bill has been built up few months after the death of the CEO/Chair. If the board happened to fix the apartment, the board may not do any good work at it.

There is one more document that I sent just to add it to the court file if it is not too late. I happened to get access to it at the end of November 2014. It is about the Stock Certificate of my father. As I mentioned before your honor, I do not know if the Stock Certificate is real or legit. The board told me, particularly the that the Stock Certificate is mandatory to all shareholders. I send a copy of the Stock Certificate. Add the Stock Certificate in the court file if it is not too late.

Sincerely

Name omitted

Name omitted

Address omitted for the purpose of the book

(**Temporary address**)

• Did not send to Authority.

Van Hugo

From (name omitted)

Court case index: omitted

8/7/15

Name and address omitted for the purpose of the book

Letter to Judge (name omitted)

I send this letter to you to let you know that I am not appreciating about what is going on with the appeal. I have been doing all it takes to find out about the status of my appeal on Thursday August 6, 2015 and all I got from the employees on seventh floor and fifteenth floor is that there was no record of my appeal. I even got blamed from one of the employees on the seventh about that because she kept saying that I should get written transcript from the person that I choose on the list that they have. I have been told by the employee on the seventh floor that I should be the one to get the written transcript from the person I chose from the list to go to the next step, as well as be the one who should take care of that despite the fact I would pay the fees to the person who take care of the transcript. The same thing has been told to me on February 2015. I went to see the person i choose from the list that the seventh floor the same day I left seventh floor on February 2015. The person told me that she had done with everything and about to send them in. She also said that she would call which she never did. Since employee on the seventh floor told me that I supposed to be the one to get in contact with the person I chose from list most submit hard copy of transcript on seventh floor or else things will never proceeded from there. I called the person on the seventh floor on Tuesday August 4, 2015 to find out about the status of the appeal. She told me that she will call. I still never receive that phone call. I asked the employee on the seventh can she at least send letter to the person I chose from the list about the issue concerning the appeal. She blamed me by saying that it is my problem to deal with as well as my responsibility that I chose anyone from the list. However, when that list was giving to me at the end of October 2014, I asked the employees on the seventh floor who do they think that I should choose form the list. I have been told by them that it was my decision make and they were unable to help me with that. The employee on the seventh floor was ambiguous about everything that she said to me. She even said to me that "if i pay for the milk, i should get the milk" which I have no idea what this got to do with the appeal. She ended up walk out of me and made it look like I was the one who caused the problem. She even walked out on me without answering my questions, as well as if she would send a letter to the person I chose from the list concerning about the appeal. i even sent letter to the person I chose form the list about appeal twice by email and hard copy. She never sends any response. I even do not receive any response from you your Honor on the last letter I sent to you on March 2015, after I reported to you about that the board rented out the apartment under my father's name illegally.

I began to be impatient now because I have been homeless for a year and the court cannot tell me about the appeal as well as blaming me for everything. If the court know this problem is huge why the court went along with the eviction. The court could have had stopped the eviction from happening. I also want the court to know that the court must take full responsibility to find a place for me to live now. The temporary address that I live now is not a family member. The people who live in the address happen to be friends from church of my mother. They were the ones who took me and my mother in their apartment on the day the eviction took place on September 2015. I would have nowhere to go if it was for them. Fees starting to apply on us beginning of 2015 for our staying in their apartment, when they found out that this problem is huge. There is none such things as free lunch when it comes to economics. However, it seems to me that they could not keep us in their apartment anymore because we appear to be there illegally, as well as caused problem for them. Our days are numbered now. The court could not blame us for all of the problems that the board and their lawyers caused to us. What happened to us are not only prejudice, discrimination, unfairness, but also a crime and cruelty. I even do the best I could to feel out applications for apartments from few private companies and public last year (2014). I have not received any response from them yet. The court better be careful not to use anything as excuses to ignore the problems that occurred to us because the court contributed to the problem that occurred to us. The court has until Friday August the 21, 2015 to tell me what they will do with us on finding a place to live now, or else I may choose to go to the Media to report on all the discrimination, prejudice, unfairness, and perjury, that I have been face in court and out of the courtroom, the court does not do anything about them. I would report that the court let some crooked Lawyers with their clients come to the courtroom to do whatever they want as if they possess license to steal and lie. I have few of that on the report I wrote and the Justice Department knew about them. The court must also find out about the status of my appeal from the person I chose from the list that seventh floor has. The person's full name is Leah Hart. She lives a block away from the court. I chose her from the list because she lives near than anyone on the list that seventh floor has.

Sincerely

My name omitted

My name omitted

Address omitted for the purpose of the book

• Sent to Authority.

From My name omitted

Address omitted for the purpose of the book

3/07/15

To J**** A***** S******, P.C.

Address omitted for the purpose of the book

Dear J**** A***** S******, P.C.

I send this letter to let you know that I either need all my $1700 dollars that you collect from me in cash for wrong and useless work that you provided to me as an Attorney during the time I had to deal with the illegal eviction at (building address omitted). You either give all of my money back or I get at least $1500 dollars back. You provided me with a poor work and that poor work almost Jeopardize everything for me. Some of the reasons that I need my money back in cash are stated below:

The first reason I need my money back is when you read the response that the judge sent to everyone during the time I was in court with the board. You told me that it is too late to do something about the paper because I had 60 to 90 days to do something about it. You wrong because the court collected all the responses that I sent to **G***** and L***,** the time I was in court with the Board on the HP action cases that I filed against them. It was the board who brought me in court for holdover proceeding and it was the board who had 60 to 90 days to fix the mess that they have been created. The Judge did not know if the board went to Marshal for me after 90 days. I also did know if I had to be in court right away when I received the Marshal notice. I went to the Marshal office and had been told that I had to be in court right away. The Judge was surprised to see me back in court. He told me that I had to serve the board' lawyers right away because this could not wait. The board and their lawyers had to come to court a day later. The board did exactly what they did on the HP action cases. The board changed lawyers from the same law firm to represent them in court when the first lawyer who represented them stuck with everything that they did with their lawyers. The board tried to change what they represented in court. They did the same thing during the HP action case, and they did the same thing on holdover proceeding case. Their lawyers also knew about everything already. I came with all the papers that I gave in court, as well as the papers that I received from the board with me in your office. You did not ask me any of that when came to your office with them. The Judge wrote his response based on what the court collected from me before trial. For that reason and failure, I need my money back. You also did not ask me if I send response. **Do not ask, do not tell**. That was what the first Judge asked me if I send response to the board's lawyers before the case went on trial. I also had to force the board to testify against themselves in court. The board was Dumb and stupid when the judge gave them chance to walk away from the mess they had created before the trial. The Judge gave them chance to walk away from their mess. They just wanted to go on trial.

The second reason is that the way you file for the appeal was really wrong. That was not the way the appeal should be done. You sent me to the wrong floor to do the appeal. You sent me to the 15th floor to do the appeal. The appeal that you filed had been refused on the 15th floor without going to the courtroom. The appeal that you did for me had been denied by a different Judge after reviewed it. I had to start from the scratch after the mess that you created. The court sent me to a place located on Court Street. The person who handled my case almost made the same mistake that you made. The person was wondering about the response that the Judge wrote. I told him that the court collected response from me, along with the documents collected in court for the trial. He asked for the response that collected in court, not the ones that collected and signed by the Judge and sent back to me during and after the trial. I had to give same copies of the response that the court collected from me by the court. The person said that he will call which I did not receive any phone calls from the person. I had to call the person a week later and found out that the case is too complex and that was not what they did at his office. He told me that go to the 7th floor just to do the appeal. The appeal has been done the way it should be done. I also sent letter to the judge who handled the holdover proceeding case, explaining to him that have been blamed for not doing anything about the response that he sent to everyone. The paper did not say I have to anything about it. Even though their lawyers sent me papers after the trial, is also wrong because the court does not know if I receive any papers for their lawyers outside the courtroom. I want you to know that if the court asked question about bout the first appeal, I would tell the truth about that I was done by a lawyer to represent my case. I also been told by one of the officer of the court said that any clients should never go out to pay lawyers for cases like mine because they would lose their money. I that case I would not lose my money. I felt that I had been bamboozled by everything you had done for me over the case.

The third reason is that you used a Bylaws that was fake to do the appeal. I let the court knew about the Bylaws that I received by the board is faked when I took stand. I also told the board to come to court with Bylaws during the holdover proceeding, and the board did not come with the Bylaws. The Bylaws had been challenged when I sent response to the board lawyers, **G******* and L*****. I knew the Bylaws was faked in almost a month before I file for the first HP action against them. It was the board gave me the faked Bylaws. Therefore, you are being held responsible and accountable for that, as well as you asked me for the Bylaws. You did not read, review, and analyze the Bylaws. The Bylaws also reviewed by the person who was handled the case and also found out that it was faked.

I want you to know that I am not in the apartment anymore. I still use the apartment as my primary address to some degree. I use the address and not the address that I live in temporary. Only the Court knew about the temporary address that I live in. If you want send response you can just call at (omitted) or send me email at (omitted). I also want you to know that failure of not giving my money back in cash may result to send this letter along with another letter to the Justice Department explaining to them about everything. This is not a threat or warning. The law indicates that any lawyers should never collect money from their clients when the clients' cases have not been solved. You also have to know what is important, the money or you and your law firm's reputation. The choice is yours to decide. You have until 3/20/15 to decide. I also want you to know the board went against what the Judge wrote on paper. I sent this letter along with the copy of the Judge response.

Sincerely

My name omitted

• Note: sent to Authority.

From: Omitted

To: Omitted

Sent: Tuesday, March 17, 2015 1:49 PM

Subject: Your Letter dated March 7, 2015

Mr. (Last name omitted): I am in receipt of your letter referenced above and respond accordingly. In fact, I have read your letter several times, and to be blunt, I find it largely unintelligible. From what sense I can make of it, you are talking about matters that I had no part in, nor gave you any legal advice about. From my recollection, you came to my office twice (at least one of those times without making an appointment). You essentially walked in off of the street. You were not clear on how you found me or my firm. At the time, I believe you had already been evicted or were at least physically out of the apartment. You had attempted to vacate the judgment entered against you after trial, and Judge(name omitted) had already denied that application. Both my associate and I spent several hours with you, going over the facts of your case. I gave you clear advice on how things could be handled, and specifically advised you that I did not believe there was much I, or anyone, could do at this stage of the litigation, specifically in light of your attempt to vacate the judgment. I explained how an appeal was your last possibility, and also stated that I did not believe the likelihood of success on that appeal was not very good. However, after several hours of going over your matter, you insisted on going ahead with the appeal. You and I came to an agreement that I would assist you with the preparation of certain documents if you needed it but that I would not be your attorney of record. The fee arrangement we made was based on the time spent discussing your matter, strategizing, providing legal advice and assisting with your preparation of the certain documents that you could not do on your own.

I never told you there was a 60-90 day time frame to do anything. I was never involved with Go***** & L***, other than I telephoned them, while you were in my office, to arrange for access to the apartment so you could retrieve your personal items. I was never involved in any HP action. I did not tell you what floor to go file your appeal on, as I do not know what floor the Appellate Term is located in Kings County. I had no way of knowing whether by-laws were, or are, fake in our two meetings. After our 2nd meeting, I never heard from you again until this letter, months later.

Despite your statement to the contrary, your letter is absolutely a threat. It serves no other purpose than to attempt to scare me into paying you money that there is no valid reason to pay you for. I am confident that I gave you good legal advice, and assisted you to the best of my ability. Then I never heard from you again. I do not know, or from your letter even understand, what you did with that advice. If you had an issue with something I told you, then it would have been prudent to advise me at the time so I could clarify. Now, many months later, it is impossible for me help you any further.

J**** A***** S******, P.C.

Attorney At Law

address omitted for the purpose of the book

E-MAIL NOTICE-This transmission may be: (1) subject to the Attorney-Client Privilege, (2) an attorney work product, or (3) strictly confidential. If you are not the intended recipient of this message, you may not disclose, print, copy or disseminate this information. If you have received this in error, please reply and notify the sender (only) and delete the message. Unauthorized interception of this e-mail is a violation of federal criminal law.

• Note: send to Authority.

From: Omitted

To: Omitted

Sent: Tuesday, March 17, 2015 5:44 PM

Subject: Re: Your Letter dated March 7, 2015

J**** A***** S******, P.C.

Attorney At Law

address omitted for the purpose of the book

March 17, 2015

Van Hugo

To J**** A***** S******

I send this response to you to let you know that you are a liar just like G***** and L*** because that was what G***** and L*** did in court. They kept lying about everything. You specifically told me I had 60 to 90 days to do something about that and the time was just passed. I wish I could just record all of the conversation on my phone while I came to your office if I knew you would lie about everything. Another lawyer told me about the same thing when I paid him a visit a week after I came to visit you. He almost charged me the same amount that you had charged me ($1500) and said almost the same thing that you said to me. That was when I began to be a little suspicion about what was going on. I was not going to come to your office, I told you that a shareholder who you represented in court, recommended me to come to see you when I came to your office. You can look at my letter as blunt and unintelligible all you want. As I said before, you have up until 3/20/15 just to give me my money back. Another thing, I do not think you are recognized by the court because you and some other law firms just like G***** and L*** just take money from your clients and leave them with the mess. No wonder why G***** and L*** is in trouble along with their clients. You do not give any legal or good advice to me. You just provided me with a shitty or worthless service and asked me to pay huge amount money for it. That was also your job as a lawyer to find out if the Bylaws was fake or real. I knew from the day I received the bylaws from the board and found out it was faked. As I mentioned in the letter that I sent to you «do not ask, do not tell». The choice is yours again. You have to find out which one is more important to you; my money or your reputation and your law firm›s reputation. What you just send to me can be used against you in the court of law. I found it surprise that you send this email to me. You can use all the fancy words you want to judge my letter. Fancy words are just meaningless and useless to me. You did not hear from me because I was waiting to see how the appeal would turn out and found out that it is a long process, as well as the way it should be done. The court sent me all of the recordings that took place in court. You will be surprised what is in the recordings as well as my response. No wonder why you let me go off alone to do all the work in court when actually it was you who should have done all the work. I paid you to do all the work. Paying a lawyer $1700 for not doing anything is unfair and unacceptable. You also knew for facts that the appeal was not going to work the way you had done it. Like you said I had a small chance that the appeal would work. You also said that you do not want to feel guilty to take my money. You also do not provide me with a receipt of payment I made after you charged me. As I already mentioned before, I have been bamboozled by you. I thought you were different, and I am very disappointed by you.

Sincerely

my name omitted

my name omitted

Address omitted for the purpose of the book

Case against J**** A***** S******, P.C.

Send to J**** A***** S******, P.C. by email on (3/21/15) after ignoring the deadline on 3/20/15 to do something about the problem.

Note: I want you to know that if I happen to send the case I have against you and your Law Firm to Authority, and have been told to go to the Supreme Court, you will end up paying more for bringing you to court. I had been in the Supreme Court already, and it is costly to go there. We can deal with this problem without the involvement of the Government and/or the Court. It is going to be very painful for me, especially for you if either or both the Justice Department and the Supreme Court get involve in the case. I also want you to know that there are more problems in the response that you sent to me, after you receive the letter that I sent to you along with the copy of the Judge decisions. I want you to know that I have cases against you for being careless, arrogant, ignorant, irresponsible and use me as scapegoat (or patsy) after you read the response I sent to you. See below:

- The few of the problems that you stated that you never told me that I had 60 to 90 days to do something about the Judge response and that time had passed. You happened to be the first person whom I came to first before I went somewhere else. You also told me that the Judge was wrong after you read the second response. You also told me that it was the Judge who kicked me out and his decision was wrong. It was you who asked me about the envelopes sent by G***** and L*** after the Judge sent response to everyone individually. I found it surprised that G***** and L*** sent me the same response that the Judge sent to everyone in four envelopes. You told me that you need these envelopes. I told you that the envelopes had been locked in the apartment on the day Marshal came to get us out of the apartment. You called G***** and L*** and told them that I would come to get my belongings out of the apartment. You also said to me that I must come with the envelopes sent by G***** and L***, with the payment. That was the only thing you did well for me about getting my belongings out of the apartment because the board threw the rest of our stuff out, fix the apartment, and rented under my father's name for 1700 dollars.

You told me that the Judge was wrong and the case should go to the Supreme Court. You also said that the Judge who handled the case was a small Judge. You told me that I had a small chance that the appeal might work and you do not want to feel guilty about taking my money. You also told me that if the appeal went through, came back to you to represent me to the Supreme Court, and you would charge me another fee that was higher than the first fee. You also said to me that represent in court would embarrassed for you because the Judge would ask you that you know what is going on in the response that he sent and it was useless, worthless, and wasting time for you to represent me in court. You called your Associate to prepare the court paper after you took the money from me.

I came to your office just to have few documents feeling out a day or two days later due to the fact that there were few papers that the court gave me to fill out. I called your office many times to set up an appointment for that and there was no one there to pick up the phone. I came by early one morning to have that done. You did not even welcome me well and told me that I cannot show up in your office like that. I found surprise and disrespectful of you saying that to me after you took my money. You just finished what had not been done and I went to court. The appealed had been refused by a different Judge on the floor that you sent me (15th floor).

• Other few reasons are that I have been Bamboozled and used by you because you had used a different and wicked meaning and interpretation of the Judge decisions. I began to find out that I have been doing this thing as well as dealing with them for the first time, and found ways to take advantage of me. I had been doing some research about everything after dealing with you and the others. I began to get some clarity about what has been going. You never told me that the board and their lawyers G***** and L*** went against the Judge's decision. As for the Bylaws, it was your responsibility to find out if it was real or fake. As I said before, do not asked do not tell. You just told me if I had the Bylaws with me. You just flipped pages and you asked your associate to write something that came from the fake Bylaws and put it on the appeal that you and your associate filled out. I was surprised that you use the Bylaws without reviewed and analyzed to see if it was real or fake. Blaming me for the fake Bylaws is unfair and unacceptable because it was your responsibility to find out if it was real or fake. Do not use me as a scapegoat (or patsy) about the Bylaws. Even the board and their lawyers (G***** and L***) trapped with the Bylaws because the Bylaws had been challenged not only during the HP action cases, but also on the Holdover Proceeding case.

Since you claimed that you give me advice which was not because you tried to make matter worst for me. As I mentioned to you before, one of the court officers had been told not to go spending money on lawyers in cases like mine because the clients would lose their money. Since you claimed that you give advice, you have to prove was your advised was good ones or bad ones. Based on what had been happened to me here, your advised count as bad advice. Therefore, I had been victimized by you and your advice.

Since you stated that you did not tell me what floor to go to file my appeal, as you do not know where the Appellate Term is located in Kings County caused two problems for you. The first problem is that you denied saying that you did not know where it is located, then who told me. It was you who told me that go to the 15th floor just to get the next step done. That step had to do about served the board's lawyer(s) because I had to serve them to let them knew that I began an appeal against them. The second problem is that you took my money to fill out for an appeal and you do not know where the Appellate Term is located. That is very wrong of you. You sounded like a blind man leading another blind man. As I mentioned to you before it was your job to do all the paperwork without having me going around doing them when I paid you huge amount of money without doing anything. I should have charged you fees for doing your job. I look at what you did to me not only unfair, but also like a slave or subordinated.

It was wrong to charge me for something that the court knew about already. As I mentioned to you before that you did not even want to take a look at my exhibit, as well as the board's exhibit. That was the last part the Judge put on his decision and you completely ignored it. I came to your office with the envelop that the Judge sent to us, along with the documents collected in court before the trial to your office during the times I came to your office. You ignored that. You also ignored everything that the Judge puts on paper and went only after one thing. You went after the one that you have marked on the Judge decision. You will see on the one that you had marked on the Judge decision is in my response collected in court before the trial. It was from my response collected in court the Judge wrote his decision. You blamed me for not doing anything when I actually did.

Note: I never receive any response from the Authority. I went to the place and delivered the case by hand. Another case I had also delivered by hand at the same place. I have not heard from anyone about the result of them.

Bonus Part

Anonymous, serious problem in NYC Housing

I t was early April 2017 when my mother's friend daughter broke the news to me that she would no longer took money from me for the bedroom, which was not a bedroom, anymore. She said that she wanted me and my mother to leave by the end of July 2017. I knew this was going to happen. She did so because my mother's personality cannot be tolerated anymore. However, some of the accusations towards my mother were false. As I mentioned about my mother is a stubborn person. She never listen and has no understanding about people can use anything against her, if she never being careful around people. They even accused me of things that I did not do despite that I have been very careful with them. One of the accusations was dumb and stupid. I began to find out that they caused some actions on purpose and blamed me for them, even though they knew that I knew they wrong and never seemed to apologize to me about them. I do not blame them for anything that they did toward me and my mother. I also do not blame them for not accepting us anymore in their apartment. I knew this day would come because they started to give us hard time in almost a year after the eviction took place. This also proves how poorly the system is when dealing with tenants looking for apartment. I did what I could to get an apartment (a room since apartments seem to become unaffordable now), as well as reached out to the Judge who held the trial of the holdover proceeding by letters the third time. The court seemed to be careless and left me and my mother neglected. The letters also concern about the appeal again. The court never send response to me concerning about the appeal.

I did what I could to get room for both of us and hope for the best. I also knew that it will be difficult to get something for both of us because my mother is on social security. I let my mother knew that I may not find something for both of us after I broke the news to her about her friend and her daughter would no longer wanted us to stay in their apartment. She listened to some degree because she would get affected by decision that would come later. It is going to be difficult for anyone to get apartment if they do not have income, particularly good and stable income.

Therefore some people in the city are actually facing some kind financial discrimination to get apartments or rooms. I went to online to do some research about renting an apartment or room. However, it was shocking to see huge prices on both. It seemed to be that people with income range of $20000-$30000 unable to find one bedroom or two bedroom apartments. It is also even hard to get a room with this income range to some degree. The first website I checked, I filled out information that was needed from me. However, I found out that the people do not really help me. They wanted me to call the real estate to get the room. I would pay them a fee if I get the room. This is ridiculous to pay someone while I do all of the work. I got in contact with the owner of the real estate. I even set up an appointment to come to see him. However, I met with the employees of the owner. They interviewed me and found out from them that the room I wanted to rent from them was not opened to new tenant because the tenant somehow extended the contract with them. They even asked me questions about the reason why I want to rent the room from them. Some of the questions had to about invading in my privacy that concerns the building I lived in. I could not lie but telling them the truth. However the truth seemed to be spooked them. I still not have the expectation that I will get the room. I told them that I need the room for me and my mother. I even told them I would pay the price they charged for the room per month when I told them that my mother is on social security. I kept checking other websites as well, particularly "naked" and "trulia" meanwhile. These website only have room available for only one person. The owner kept making empty promises that he would get me a room and he was not forgotten about me.

At the end of April 2017, he called me criminal indirectly and committed injustice against me because he did not give rooms to anyone who had been evicted. The owner wanted to find out about the court decision. I decided to send all the court decision about the holdover proceeding case, along with my response and the cards I received from the court by email. However the second place I checked was from a student who was an engineering major at City College, who turned out to become real estate broker. I met with him probably on November 2016, not far away from the buildings I was evicted. I explained to him what I had to go through. He gave me his card. I called him on the second or third week of April 2017. He also wanted to find out about the court decision. I send everything to him by email before I sent them to the real estate owner who treated me like a criminal. I had a feeling that he was unable to help me because I did not hear from him after he received the court case along with my response by email. It seemed to me that both real estates concerned more about knowing where I live and tried to do some business with the buildings. I warned him about the buildings I evicted from is a Co-Op. He ignored me and told me that I lost the apartment forever. He also told me that my father should give me power of attorney. He even added that the court decision is nothing because the landlords can still do whatever they want. He said that was what some landlords said to him. I warned both of them by email, telling them that the buildings I was evicted from is handoff and there is no landlord. No wonder I did not rely heavily on them about getting a room or one bedroom apartment.

I checked some of the buildings near the building I was evicted from and made some phone calls. I called on of them one Saturday morning. I spoke with someone on the phone and told me that they do not have anything below $1000. The person on the phone told me that she can do her best to find out if I can get a studio. She told me to come to fill out an application. I decided to go the same day. I met with her and she wanted to find out the reason why I was evicted. I told her that I was evicted under perjury, identity theft, and falsified information and document. She was surprise that I live in a Co-Op and told me briefly about problems that happened in the Co-Ops. Last time I checked Landlords are the worse to deal with. One can find it is beneficial to live in a Co-Op (refer to HDFC Co-Op) than living in the buildings control by landlords. No wonder why the board of the buildings I was evicted from illegally behaves like landlords. The board did so because they looking for total dominion over the shareholders and have the right not to pay anything for over twenty years. I wonder if anyone wonder how the landlords pay their personal bills.

There was one of the people I spoke with who happened to be a coworker told me that the landlords owed so much money to the tenants. She may have a point there. Otherwise she may be mistaken. She used to go to the housing court to debate cases against her landlord. I found strange that majority of the buildings in New York City should not turned into HDFC Co-Ops, particularly those built from 1900 until 1970. I checked another real estate place, one block away from where my mother's friend lives. I checked the price on the apartment and found out that the price range for apartment is $1500 and up. I spoke with one of the person who worked there since he was alone. He told me that the place did not do rental in rooms. He added that the real estate is the middle man for the landlord because they help the landlord to find tenants for their buildings. He added that it is wrong and unfair to raise rent so high in apartments. I hope he meant what he said.

I checked online to find addresses about places. I went to a place on Amsterdam, near the area of City College. I asked them if there is anything available in Brooklyn, particularity for two people. They told me that they do Queens and Manhattan. They told me that they only find rooms for individuals, not couples. A week later, I receive a text from one of the website I checked. I went there for an interview and I have been tricked to give $150. The people in there knew for facts that they have been doing some monkey business. They also make their policy about no refund. They told me to pay first before they start the process. I found it strange that they send me to a website created by them, to call as many building owners as possible to get a room. That was not what they send to me on the text. The text said that they will help me found a room. I ended up paid fees and do all the work my own. This place was not the only place done that to me. Another place sent me an email for an interview to get an apartment. I went there they told me that they help people with any sort of income. I paid another fee, nearly $150. They told me that they will help me to find an apartment. However, they send me email every Tuesday and Friday concerning about apartments available in Brooklyn and Queens. Everything is over a thousand dollars per month. There was only one place that used to be about $ 850 a month for one bedroom apartment. I called and been told to go only to download the application. It took me nearly a month and half later to send my application after I found out from the person who sent the email to me said that they do not help me to get the apartment, I must called the owners myself. However, it was too late because I received a letter along with the money orders I sent stated that they could not find anything for me and my mother. I even called them to get confirmation on that. I hoped that anything have been used as excuses, pretext, or advantage to prevent me from getting the apartment, just like the first place I went to on May 2016. I do not have a proprietary lease and landlord to send information about.

I kept doing my research and applied for room. I did not include my mother because I turned down on rooms available for only one person. There was one place promised to call me when they found a room for me and my mother, but never call me back. One of the places I checked was on Broadway junction. It was kind of far for me and my mother. I set up an appointment with owner. I went to the place and found out that the place was under renovation. The owner told me to give deposit down and expected to open the place in May 2017, if she gets as many renters she needed as possible for the whole place. The room is small and the floor is not made of wood. She charged me over eight hundred per month. I told her I would call her. I received another text or email concerning about renting room at prospect place. I set up an appointment with someone I thought was the owner. However they were two female roommates who tried to rent a small room in their apartment for eight hundred a month. One of them was a Caucasian; the other one who came to open the door at the lobby for me to come in was probably mix of race. Her complexion was the same as the female character that the just added recently on the Fast and Furious movies. The female character that Tyrese and Ludacris had triangle love for. The roommate hair style was that of the female actress from the Fast and Furious movies. The room they were about rent is very small. The bed took most of the place. The whole apartment is smaller than the one I evicted from. The building is very old. The building has been built during the 1900. I asked them if they are rented apartments in the building. They told me yes. They told to get the information when I got out of the building. I did and called the place many times. Therefore no one seemed to pick up or even called me back.

One day, early May 2017, I received an email and text about the same address from either Trulia or Naked after I saw advertisement about one bedroom available for rent at the same address for $ 800 per month. However it was not true. There was a room renting on another address, not on the one that I apply for. There was a mistake on the advertisement on the one that I applied for. I spoke with the lady on the phone about that when she called me. She told me that there is no bedroom in New York City at the price range $700 anymore; otherwise I should get out of New York. I set up an appointment with the agent after I wasted my time waiting on the first appointment I had with him on a room that should be renting in an apartment inhabited by a tenant located between. The lady I spoke with on the phone, game me the wrong number of the address I should go to meet with the agent. It was the agent who told me over the phone the right number of the building to come to see the apartment. I took the C train and I approach the building. It is an old building that was built in 1910's when I check information about it. The agent and I went in the apartment and I checked the two rooms that were available. I chose one of them. The agent told me to make the deposit of $775 dollars quick because there are others that are interested to get the room. One of the clients already took one room. The agent told me that it will be only three roommates in the apartment and one room would be the living room. I checked all of the rooms and found out that two had closets and the other two did not have closet. I made the transaction. I paid the $775 dollars on my credit card and the application fees. On the middle of May, I have been told to pay another $775 dollars for May and June 2017 rent. It was the lady I spoke with on the phone I went to see at the office one Sunday afternoon.

The lady told me that I have to pay for rent before they gave me the key to the apartment. I have been told I could either pay by check or credit card. They never told me about if money order is fine or not, until I came with a post office money order. They had no choice but to accept it. However something was not right. I replied to the agent I met to show the apartment to give the full name of the landlord and the full address of where I should send money on rent. The agent never replied to my email after he sent me email about to pay monthly rent R**** P***** Realty LLC. The Real Estate office was unable to give the address but only told me to follow what the agent told me to follow. That is kind of weird and strange to send money to someone or place when there is no address provide to me. The people at the Real Estate office wanted to help me make the payment, which I know that it was not for free because I paid another fees on my credit cards for the deposit.

I ran my own investigation and find out that there is no R**** P***** Realty LLC, but only P***** R**** Realty LLC. I kept the information that I found and hold on to them. I did not move in the room throughout the month of May because I did not completely trust what the Real Estate office told me, as well as I have not get my belonging out of my mother's friend apartment. I got the key from them I went to get the apartment twice before I move my stuff in. On May 27, 2017 late at night, my older brother helped me moved in. The lock at the apartment's door had been changed. The Real Estate and the Management of the building did not even call and told me about that. I was kind of mad about that. I called the lady and it seemed to her that it was a little joked for her by the way she was sounded on the phone. She told me to come back to the office to get another key from her the next day. I did come to get another key from her which turned out to be the wrong key. She had to call another roommate who was already move in the apartment probably in the mid of May, to come to open the door for me. The lady told me that another roommate who just moved in happened to be in the same situation as me. When I got to the apartment to check the room I chose, and found out it was already taken by the other roommate. I have been tricked by the lady when she asked me which room I chose. I gave the wrong answer. I partially blamed myself for that. It was fine by me anyway. I also found out that four people live in an apartment paying over $3000 dollars per month on rent in total. There were three African-American and one Caucasian live in the apartment.

I already told my mother that I will do my best to bring her in and she had to be prepared for anything that would cause her to get out. Therefore that was what happened. The other roommates went to report to the Real Estate office nearly a week after I moved in, about me and my mother. I had no choice after the Real Estate office told me that my mother must go, otherwise I would be evicted from the apartment. I received the phone calls while I was at work. I found it not shocking that I live among bunch of hypocrites. I would never go to snitch on them like that if they have their boyfriends, girlfriends, or family members come to stay with them. They lady even told me that I took advantage of the others and they do not like that. The lady also told me that I should have told her about my mother so that she could find something for both of us, which was not true. They only do roommates (one person per room). I chose the apartment to be free from smoking. The same must applied to everyone. However that was not what happened few months later someone has been smoking cigarettes and marijuana. The smell of them sometime gets in my room even though I close it. The filthiness is another problem. Some of them clean after using in the kitchen and bathroom improperly. While one does not clean at all, seems to think that someone would clean their mess. I really got to everyone after one of them accused me wrongfully on the texts that I received from them. I let them know that I was the only who cared so much about the apartment, and not once one of them would pick a broom and mop to clean it.

I used to clean the apartment once a week along with my room on Fridays right after work. I stopped doing that because I came home late sometime on Fridays. I did the best I can to clean the apartment once every two weeks. Above all, it was not such a bad place to live because I get peace of mind, a little freedom, and the apartment is under our responsibility. I hope they come into their senses. It has been three years since I feel that way. However there were two problems that were still remained. The first problem was that management of the building wanted to charge over $200 dollars and claimed that I moved in the room May 24, 2017. That was what the Real Estate Company told them. They will never get that money from me because they would commit corruption, extortion, and robbery. It is also illegal to charge tenant of full and partial of money for rent at the end of a month. I have been there with management twice over that issue and told them to bring me in court to prove to me why I should pay such money. That is also illegal to charge someone for a service that the person never gets. That was the reason why I did not trust the Real Estate Company because they sound so good to be true when they told me I could move in the room in May 2017. I told management to go to the Real Estate to get the money.

The second problem is that the Management of the building never gives me the name of the Landlord either. I do not even know the full names of the people who worked for management and the super. I sent a letter to them along with some evidence of what I found that there were two different mail boxes for Pacific Ralph Realty LLC when I send the second money order for rent. The letter covers about some inquiries about the charge for May, location of the management, and the Landlord's name. I also did some research and found out from an article about that thousands of building owners happened to use one address (address omitted) in Brooklyn to run their buildings. The place is not offices, but only mailboxes (maybe private mailboxes). I met with a friend of my brother who used to come to see my brother before I was evicted illegally from the apartment. He was one of the Haitians I spoke about my problem that I had to go to. I met with in almost a month after I moved in the room, one Thursday night I left the gym. He did not remember about that I told him I was evicted. I showed him the proof and the letter that I sent out to both addresses. He told me that he suffered the same problem to because he asked management of his building about the landlord because he wanted to speak with the Landlord. The management of his building never gave him an answer.

He even told me that he went to court because the Landlord told him that he owed money on rent. He told me that he went to his bank to get record of the checks. There was something similar that he faced in court from the Landlord's lawyer, which I faced twice from the board's lawyer on second HP action case and Holdover proceeding case before trials. He told me that the landlord's lawyer called him out few minutes before he saw the Judge. The lawyer told him that he should leave, do not stay. He felt strange and overwhelmed when he approached the Judge. He wondered if he made mistake for not doing anything about the problem. I also find out the reason why some people do not want to accept Post Office money order because they do not want to get track down easily. They want to remain anonymously while maximizing profits and leave big mess behind. I get scared every day because I do not want one day I came in the apartment and lock change, which lead me to stay out even though I paid on time and never miss out. I also get scared because the building had been in court on trial. The mails had been remained beside the mailboxes for anyone to see. The building also needs renovation instead of repairs because the building is filthy. The paint that they used to paint the stairs partially faded. The walls have marks all over them. Some of the apartments may not get maintenance. The apartment also has mice and few roaches. One of the roommates had to buy mice traps. I witness two mice had been caught on the traps. The neighbor(s) above me make noises all the time. On Sunday morning of October 22, 2017, the knob of the lobby door was messed up and anyone could not get out. A neighbor who lived on floor above me told me that she had spent an hour trying to get the door opened. She waved at a passerby for help. I saw the passerby while I went downstairs to get out. I went upstairs to get tape so that I can tape to knob, to keep the door from closing. Otherwise the others would get trap in the building as well. The neighbor and I were on our way to catch the train that morning. We spoke about the issue at play. I witnessed her called the super to report about the problem. The super gave her a phone number to call a person. When she did, the person did not pick up, but the person call back few minutes later. We both shocked when the person said to her that he did not know the super and unable to come for the problem. I spoke with the lady who lived on the first floor while I came in the building the next day on the afternoon. She told me that she called police and being wild on the people who are in charge of the building. I told her that I sent email as well to explain about the problem. I also let her knew that is was I who placed tape on the door knob to keep it from closing. Therefore, I cannot wait to get out of the apartment despite of all of these problems that had been happening. There may be other problem that will happen in the future. These problems will remain to be seeing. I do not use the address of the building as my current address because I just considered it as private shelter. I keep looking for apartment on both public and private, particularly private since public seems not to do about my condition, and hope for the best. I also have to go through problems for jobs that I apply on private and government job, particularly government job, because they do not want anyone use P.O. Box as addresses. Therefore I am in limbo for getting an apartment and getting a stable job in the city that is becoming very expensive unfairly. I also do not hope that the owner(s) of the building raise the room I rent from them in the future. I only live there because I have no choice. I was desperate to find a place to live despite the fact that I overpaid for it.

Sent letter to these addresses

Both addresses are omitted for the purpose of the book.

7/6/17

To P***** R**** Realty LLC

I send this letter on the behalf of management or owner of P***** R**** Realty LLC concerning about the June 2017 rent payment of $775 dollars I made by money order, for the room I rent at (address omitted). I never get any full address to endorse money to the place from the real estate that helped get the place or the management of the company. The agent of the real estate I met told me to send money to R**** P***** Realty LLC without gave the borough and zip code of the place. I did ask for it and never gave it to me. I checked only and found only P***** R**** Realty LLC located at (address omitted). I began to face problem from someone by the name D***. I told that person I need what train goes to the address. D*** told me the G train goes to near the address. D*** told me that she or he would live at 5pm. It was already too late not only the place was far from the address, but also look for the place. I got there nearly 5:30 pm and found out it place of mailboxes. I assume that Suite 1000 is box 1000. I sent email to explain everything to D*** and still blame me for something that was not my fault to begin with. He told me I should endorse money order or check to "all y**** m***** LLC" at the same address suite (address omitted). If any of you affiliated with "all y**** m***** LLC", send me back the money order on the addresses indicate below. I suggest that the money order sent to my P.O. Box (address omitted). Even D*** said it does not matter which management I sent the money because they are the same company by email. I hope to hear from anyone of you.

I want all of you to know that what you did to me is unfair and unacceptable. All of seemed to blame me for something that was not my fault. I only get information from the agent about sending money order to "R**** P***** Realty LLC", without giving me the full address. I did ask him about it, but he never replied to my email. The agent never mentioned anything about "all year management" to me. I went to the place on 7/3/17 at approximately 5:25 pm to drop the money order at (address omitted). I went to the place at approximately 5:20 pm trying to get the envelope I placed the money order. I found out from the employee that helped me out that the envelope had been picked up early after he checked the box I dropped the envelope in and the box # 1000. He asked my full name and phone number in case if he received the envelope. I told him that he could drop in box # 693, otherwise called me if he wanted me to come to pick up the envelope. There is camera (s) in the place to prove everything. He was shocked when I showed him proof of the name of the places and the place had two different box numbers. He wondered if both places affiliated to each other. The employee told me that he knew the person for box # 1000.

I send everything that I found to both addresses and boxes to all of you. Doing so is a way that none of you would say that you did not know, even though all of you seemed to know but pretend that you did not know. I also want to know all of your full names and the full names of the landlord (s). All of you know about me; particularly invaded to my privacy to get a room. I want you to know that I cannot pay the amount of $775 a month in my credit card due to the limits I have on it. That amount you ask me to pay per month will affect other payments and purchase on my credit card. As for my bank account, forget about it. I want to know why payment with money order seems to be problem or issue here.

Sincerely

My name omitted

My name omitted

Address omitted

Printed in the United States
By Bookmasters